The
Connell Guide
to

_____

Winston Churchill

_____

by
Paul Addison

Contents

Introduction   1

The early years   5
How did the young Churchill achieve so
much so quickly?   5

From MP to Cabinet minister   13
Did Churchill have a political ideology?   13
Why did he abandon the Tory party?   16
What did he achieve as a social reformer?   18
Why did Churchill move back to the right?   23
What did Churchill think about votes for
women?   26

The First World War   32
Was Churchill to blame for Gallipoli?   32

The interwar years   42
How did Churchill's world-view change
after World War One?   42
How much of a blunder was the return to
the gold standard?   45

The rise of Hitler and World War Two   52
How credible was Churchill as the "Prophet
in the Wilderness" of the 1930s?   52
How did Churchill become prime minister?   61
How did he establish himself in power?   65

government to serve on the Western Front.

1916 January 1, takes command of 6th battalion of Royal Scots in Belgium, but returns to Britain in May to resume his political career. In December David Lloyd George becomes prime minister.

1917 Churchill appointed Minister of Munitions.

1918 11 November Armistice ends the Great War.

1919 Churchill becomes Secretary of State for War and Air.

1921 As Secretary of State for the Colonies, presides at the Cairo Conference to settle Middle Eastern boundaries. In December he helps to negotiate the Irish Treaty.

1922-25 Lloyd George's coalition falls, with Churchill out of office and then in November defeated at Dundee in the general election. Other elections defeats follow until he is finally successful as the Constitutionalist candidate for Epping in 1924. Stanley Baldwin appoints him Chancellor of the Exchequer.

1931 Resigns from the shadow cabinet over Indian independence. In December he is hit by a car and badly injured in New York.

1932 Roosevelt elected US President.

1933 Hitler becomes Chancellor of Germany.

1934-5 Churchill calls for air rearmament in the House of Commons and continues his attacks on the India Bill. In October 1935 Mussolini, invades Abyssinia.

1936 Germany reoccupies the Rhineland and civil war breaks out in Spain. In December Churchill, who supports Edward VIII in the Abdication crisis, is shouted down in the Commons.

1937 28 May Baldwin resigns and Neville Chamberlain becomes prime minister.

1938 Anthony Eden resigns as Foreign Secretary in February; in March Hitler proclaims the Anschluss, the union of Austria with Germany; in September, Chamberlain signs the Munich Agreement transferring the German-speaking Sudetenland area of Czechoslovakia to Germany.

1939 10 March Hitler occupies the remainder of Czechoslovakia. 3 September, Britain declares war on Germany and Churchill is appointed First Lord of the Admiralty.

1940 Germany invades Denmark and Norway in April. Britain's response, the Norway campaign, leads to a Commons debate in May – which in turn provokes a political crisis. On 10 May, the same day Germany invades Belgium and Holland, Churchill becomes Prime Minister and Minister of Defence and forms all-party Coalition. In late May and early June thousands of British and French soldiers are evacuated from Dunkirk. In August Churchill and Roosevelt agree the destroyers-for-bases agreement.

1941 In March, Churchill sends British forces to Greece but they are defeated. On 22 June Germany invades Russia. On 7 December the Japanese attack Pearl Harbor, bringing America into the war. On 26 December Churchill addresses Congress.

1942 15 February Singapore falls to Japan; 21 June, Tobruk falls to the Germans; in August Churchill flies to Cairo to reorganise the Middle East command, then attends a conference in Moscow with Stalin. In October the Second Battle of Alamein marks the "turn of the tide" of the British war in the desert.

1943 In January, at Casablanca, Churchill and Roosevelt meet the British and American military chiefs. On 2 February the German Fifth Army is annihilated at Stalingrad. In July the Allies invade Sicily and then, in September, southern Italy. Churchill attends the Teheran Conference with Roosevelt and

Stalin at the end of November and the following month contracts pneumonia at Tunis and nearly dies.

1944 Anglo-American landings at Anzio in Italy, followed by the Allied liberation of Rome. On 6 June the Allies invade Normandy on D-Day. Paris is liberated in August.

1945 Malta Conference with Roosevelt, then the Yalta Conference with Roosevelt and Stalin. Roosevelt dies on 12 April; Hitler commits suicide in Berlin on 30 April. On 8 May, Germany surrenders. On 26 July, Churchill resigns as prime minister after landslide Labour victory in the General Election. In August America drops two atomic bombs on Japan and Japan surrenders.

1946 In March Churchill makes his "Iron Curtain" speech at Fulton Missouri; in September he talks about a "United States of Europe" in Zurich.

1951 26 October becomes prime minister for a second time.

1952 6 February death of George VI and accession of Elizabeth II. 4 November, Eisenhower elected President.

1953 In January, Churchill visits President Truman and President-elect Eisenhower in Washington. In June he has a serious stroke, which is kept secret. In December, he attends a conference with Eisenhower in Bermuda. He is also awarded the Nobel Prize for Literature.

1955 5 April resigns as Prime Minister.

1963 US Congress votes to confer honorary citizenship on Churchill.

1965 24 January Churchill dies at 27 Hyde Park Gate. 30 January, state funeral and burial at Bladon in Oxfordshire.

ENDNOTES

1. Geoffrey Best, *Churchill: A Study in Greatness* (2001), p. 336.

2. Max Hastings, *Finest Years: Churchill as Warlord 1940-45* (2010), p. 598.

3. John Charmley, *Churchill: The End of Glory* (1993), p. 649.

4. Nigel Knight, *Churchill: The Greatest Briton Unmasked* (2008), p 366.

5. Winston S. Churchill, *My Early Life* (1944 edition), p. 19.

6. Sir Gerald Woods Wollaston, 'Churchill at Harrow', in Charles Eade (ed), *Churchill by his Contemporaries* (1953), p. 19.

7. Shane Leslie, *Long Shadows* (1966), p. 21.

8. Randolph S. Churchill, *Winston S Churchill Vol I: Youth 1874-1900* (1966), p. 197, Lord Randolph to Winston 9 August 1893.

9. Martin Gilbert, *Churchill: A Life* (1991), p. 49.

10. J.B. Atkins, *Incidents and Reflections* (1947), p122.

11. Randolph S. Churchill, *Winston S. Churchill Volume I: Youth 1874-1900* (1966), p. 283.

12. Lord Moran, *Winston Churchill: The Struggle for Survival 1940-1965* (1966), p. 167.

13. Mary Soames (ed), *Speaking for Themselves: The Personal Letters of Winston and Clementine Churchill* (1998), p. 53, Winston to Clementine 11 July 1911.

14. Moran, *Winston Churchill*, p. 745 See also: Wilfred Attenborough, *Churchill and the 'Black Dog' of Depression: Reassessing the Biographical Evidence of Psychological Disorder* (2014).

15. Martin Gilbert, *In Search of Churchill* (1994), p. 210.

16. Randolph S Churchill, *Winston S Churchill Vol I: Youth 1874-1900* (1966), p. 318, Churchill to Lady Randolph 6 April 1897.

17. Paul Addison, *Churchill on the Home Front 1900-1955* (1992), p.26.

18. A.G Gardiner *Prophets Priests & Kings* (1914), p.234.

19. For the relationship between Churchill and Lloyd George see Richard Toye, *Lloyd George and Churchill: Rivals for Greatness* (2007).

20. Robert Rhodes James, *Churchill: A Study in Failure 1900-1939* (1973 edition), pps 32-3.

21. Robert Rhodes James (ed), *Winston S Churchill: His Complete Speeches Vol I* (1974), p. 1030, speech at Dundee, 4 May 1908.

22. Gilbert, *In Search of Churchill*, p. 175.

23. BBC TV, *The Long Street: The Road to Pandy Square* (1965), interview with Will H Mainwaring, accessed via YouTube.

24. Addison, *Churchill on the Home Front*, p. 130.

25. Martin Gilbert, *Never Despair: Winston S. Churchill 1945-1965* (1988), p. 308.

26. Robert Rhodes James (ed),*Winston S Churchill: His Complete Speeches Vol II 1908-1913*, p. 1587, speech of 12 July 1910.

27. Christopher Sykes, *Nancy: The Life of Lady Astor* (1972), p. 208.

28. Carlo D'Este, *Warlord: A Life of Winston Churchill At War, 1874-1945* (2009), p.445.

29. Winston S. Churchill, *The Second World War: Their Finest Hour* (1949), p. 15.

30. David Lloyd George, *War Memoirs Vol III* (1934), pp1067, 1071-2

31. Robert Rhodes James (ed), *Winston S. Churchill: His Complete Speeches Vol III 1914-1922* (1974), p. 2771, speech of 11 April 1919.

32. Rhodes James (ed), *Complete Speeches III*, p. 3119, speech of 14 July 1921.

33. Robert Skidelsky, *John Maynard Keynes: The Economist as Saviour 1920-1947* (1992), p. 198.

34. Addison, *Churchill on the Home Front*, pps 247-8, Churchill to

Niemeyer 22 February 1925.

35. P.J. Grigg, *Prejudice and Judgment* (1948), pps 182-4.

36. Skidelsky, *The Economist as Saviour*, p. 203.

37. Paul Addison, *Churchill: The Unexpected Hero* (2005), pps 96-7

38. Richard Overy, 'German Air Strength 1933-1939. A Note,' Historical Journal 27, 1984, p 469.

39. Robert Rhodes James, *Churchill: A Study in Failure 1900-1939* (1973), p.433.

40. Harold Nicolson, *Diaries and Letters 1930-1939*, ed. Nigel Nicolson (1966), p. 332, diary for 16 March 1938.

41. *Ibid*, p. 328, diary for 2 March 1938.

42. Harold Nicholson, *Diaries and Letters 1930-1939*, edited Nigel Nicholason (1970) p.328, Harold Nicholson to Vita Sackwille-West 2 March 1928.

43. Keith Feiling, *Neville Chamberlain* (1946), p.293.

44. Robert Rhodes James (ed.), *Winston S Churchill: His Complete Speeches 1897-1963 Vol VI.* p. 6004: Leo Amery, *The Empire at Bay: The Leo Amery Diaries 1939-1945,* edited by John Barnes and David Nicholson (1988) diary for 5 October 1938.

45. Winston Churchill, *Step by Step 1936-1939* (1942) p.293, 'The Morrow of Munich' 17 November 1938.

46. House of Commons Debates vol 360, col 1150, 7 May 1940.

47. Winston S. Churchill, *The Second World War Vol I: The Gathering Storm* (1948), pps 526-7.

48. Rhodes James, *Complete Speeches V*, p. 6220, 13 May 1940.

49. Martin Gilbert, *Finest Hour: Winston S Churchill 1939-1941* (1983), pps 404, 413.

50. Hugh Dalton, *The Second World War Diary of Hugh Dalton, 1939-1945*, edited by Ben Pimlott (1986), p. 28, entry for 28 May 1940.

51. Winston S. Churchill, *The Second World War Vol II: Their Finest*

Hour (1949), p. 439.

52. Harold Nicolson, *Diaries and Letters 1939-1945*, edited by Nigel Nicolson (1970), p. 205, diary for 27 January 1942.

53. House of Commons Debates (5th series) vol 381, col 528, 2 July 1942.

54. Robert Rhodes James (ed), *Winston S. Churchill: His Complete Speeches Vol VIII*, p. 8608, 30 November 1954.

55. A.J.P. Taylor, *English History* (1975), p. 479.

56. Field Marshal Lord Alanbrooke, *War Diaries 1939-1945,* edited by Alex Danchev and Daniel Todman (2001) p. xvi.

57. David Stafford, *Churchill and Secret Service* (1997), p.189.

58. *Ibid*, pps 205-6.

59. Field Marshal Lord Alanbrooke, *War Diaries 1939-1945*, edited by Alex Danchev and Daniel Todman, p. 401. Entry for 10 May 1943.

60. Sir Ian Jacob in Sir John Wheeler Bennett (ed), *Action This Day: Working with Churchill* (1968), p. 198.

61. Hastings, *Finest Years*, pps 345-6.

62. John Grigg, *1943: The Victory that Never Was* (1980), pps 123-5.

63. David Reynolds, *The Creation of the Anglo-American Alliance 1937-1941: A Study in Competitive Co-operation* (1981), p.117.

64. Warren F. Kimball (ed), *Churchill and Roosevelt: the Complete Correspondence Vol I: Alliance Emerging October 1933 to November 1942* (Princeton, New Jersey, 1984), p. 9.

65. Jon Meacham, *Franklin and Winston: A Portrait of a Friendship* (2005), p. 5

66. John Colville, *The Fringes of Power: Downing Street Diaries 1939-1945* (1985), p.624, diary for 2 May.

67. R.W.Thompson, *Churchill and Morton* (1976), p. 30.

68. Violet Bonham-Carter, *Champion Redoubtable: the Diaries and*

Letters of Violet Bonham-Carter, 1914-1945, ed. Mark Pottle (1998), pps 312-3, diary for 1 August 1944.

69. Rhode James (ed) *Complete Speeches VI*, p.6420, broadcast of 22 June 1941.

70. *King's Counsellor: Abdication and War: The Diaries of Alan Lascelles* (2006), p. 198, diary for 2 February 1944.

71. Winston S. Churchill, *The Second World War Vol VI: Triumph and Tragedy* (1954), p. 124.

72. Mary Soames (ed), S*peaking for Themselves: The Personal Letters of Winston and Clementine Churchill* (1998), p. 506, Winston to Clementine, 13 October 1944.

73. Churchill, *The Second World War VI*, p. 252, Churchill to Scobie 5 December 1944.

74. Dalton, *Second World War Diary*, p. 836, diary for 23 February 1945.

75. Rhodes James (ed), *Complete Speeches VII*, p. 7117, speech of 27 February 1945.

76. Colville, *The Fringes of Power*, p. 565, diary for 27 February 1945.

77. Winston S. Churchill, *My African Journey* (1972 edition), p. 25.

78. Ronald Hyam, *Elgin and Churchill at the Colonial Office 1905-1908* (1968), p. 497.

79. Christopher Thorne, *Allies of a Kind: the United States, Britain and the War against Japan 1941-1945* (1978), p5.

80. Colville, *The Fringes of Power*, p. 563, diary for 23 February 1945.

81. Moran, *Winston Churchill*, p. 280, diary for 23 July 1945.

82. Rhodes James (ed), *Collected Speeches VIII*, p. 8282, speech of 23 October 1951.

83. Rhodes James (ed), *Ibid*, pps 7292-3.

84. Rhodes James (ed), *Ibid*, p 7289.

85. *New York Times*, 7 March 1946; Washington Post, 7 March 1946.

86. Peter Clarke, *Mr Churchill's Profession: Statesman, Orator, Writer* (2012), pps 117-8.

87. Winston S. Churchill, 'The United States of Europe' in Michael Wolff (ed), *The Collected Essays of Sir Winston Churchill Vol II: Churchill and Politics,* (1976), p. 184.

88. *Daily Mirror*, 25 October 1951.

89. CS VIII p 8282, 23 Oct 1951.

90. Soames (ed), *Speaking for Themselves*, p. 96, Winston to Clementine 29 July 1914.

91. Roy Jenkins, *'Churchill: the Government of 1951-1955'* in Robert Blake and William Roger Louis (ed), Churchill (1993), p. 492.

92. Robert Rhodes James, *Complete Speeches VIII*. P8629, speech of 1 March 1955.

93. Quoted in Anthony Storr, 'The Man' in A.J.P. Taylor at al, *Churchill: Four Faces and the Man* (1973), p. 213.

FURTHER READING

The official biography

The cornerstone of Churchill studies is the official biography, published in eight volumes between 1966 and 1988. The first two volumes were written by Churchill's son Randolph S Churchill and the remaining six by Martin Gilbert. Accompanying them is a series of companion volumes of documents, of which eighteen have been published to date and another five are still to come. This stupendous work provides readers with a meticulously detailed chronicle of Churchill's life, together with a vast array of the primary source materials on which it is based. While far too long for all but the most dedicated researchers, the official biography is always worth browsing and definitive on points of detail. Gilbert condensed his unrivalled knowledge of the subject into a single volume, listed below.

Paul Addison, *Churchill: The Unexpected Hero* (2005) A concise biography and a study of his transformation from political misfit to national hero.

Christopher M. Bell, *Churchill and Seapower* (2013) A scholarly revision of the record, largely in Churchill's favour.

Geoffrey Best, *Churchill: A Study in Greatness* (2001) Passionately defends Churchill while depicting him 'warts and all'.

David Carlton, *Churchill and the Soviet Union* (2000) Argues that anti-communism was his deepest and most consistently held belief.

John Charmley, *Churchill: The End of Glory* (1992) A right-wing critique of Churchill as an opportunist and failed war leader.

Peter Clarke, *Mr Churchill's Profession: Statesman, Orator, Writer (*2012) Shows how Churchill financed an extravagant way of life from the fabulous sums he earned as a writer.

Martin Gilbert, *Churchill: A Life* (1991) Hugely informative distillation of a lifetime's research but short on analysis.

Max Hastings, *Finest Years: Churchill as Warlord 1940-1945* (2009) An intensely human portrait tempering hero-worship with a military historian's insight into Churchill's failings.

Robert Rhodes James, *Churchill: A Study in Failure 1900-1939* (1973)A seminal study of the reasons why Churchill aroused so much mistrust before 1940.

Roy Jenkins, *Churchill* (2001)A well-rounded and closely observed life characterised by the profound admiration of one professional politician for the skills of another.

Warren F. Kimball, *Forged in War: Churchill, Roosevelt and the Second World War* (1997) A lucid and subtle interpretation of the rise, zenith and decline of the alliance between Prime Minister and President.

Richard M Langworth, *Churchill by Himself: The Life, Times and Opinions of Winston Churchill in his Own Words* (2008) Indispensable because it delivers exactly what the subtitle promises.

David Reynolds, *In Command of History: Churchill Fighting and Writing the Second World War* (2004) A brilliant analysis of the way in which Churchill sought to vindicate his record by imposing his own version of the past on the more complex realities of history.

David Stafford, *Churchill and Secret Service* (1997) A highly original study demonstrating Churchill's lifelong involvement with the world of secret intelligence

Richard Toye, *Churchill's Empire: The World That Made Him and the World He Made* (2010) The most comprehensive, searching and perceptive account of Churchill's imperial attitudes and policies.

INDEX

A

Abdication crisis 56–57
Aitken, Max
  see Beaverbrook, Max, 1st
  Baron
Amery, Leo 60, 63
Asquith, Herbert 14, 19, 23, 24,
  27–28, 32, 36, 41, 42
Astor, Nancy, Viscountess 31
Atkins, J.B. 9
Atomic bomb 90, 103, 116, 128
Attlee, Clement 65, 67, 105, 108,
  112

B

Baldwin, Stanley 45–46, 49–50,
  52–55, 56–57, 104, 126–127
Balfour, Arthur 15, 22
Beaverbrook, Max, 1st Baron 28,
  57
Best, Geoffrey 2
Bevan, Aneurin 70
Beveridge Report (1942)
  104–105
Bevin, Ernest 69, 108
Boer War 12, 15, 125
Bonham-Carter, Violet 91–94
Bracken, Brendan 13, 64
Briand, Aristide 111
British Empire
  decline 3, 86–87, 94, 101, 118
  proposals for Anglo-American
  alliance 109–111, 113–114,
  119–120
  and W.S.C. Imperial
  paternalism 100–102
British Gazette 49–50
Brooke, Alan, 1st Viscount 80,
  83–84

C

Campbell-Bannerman, Sir Henry
  14, 18
Chamberlain, Joseph 16–17
Chamberlain, Neville 51–53,
  57–60, 63–68, 100–101, 104, 127
Charmley, John 3

Chartwell (family home) 72, 110
Churchill, Clementine Ogilvy
  Spencer (*née* Hozier; wife;
  "Clemmie") 12–13, 27–29, 71,
  90, 98, 110, 114–115
Churchill, Diana (daughter) 28
Churchill, George Spencer, 8th
  Duke of Marlborough (uncle) 8
Churchill, Jack (brother) 118
Churchill, Jeanette (*née* Jerome;
  mother) 6, 11, 14–15, 99, 118
Churchill, John, 1st Duke of
  Marlborough 5
Churchill, Lord Randolph
  (father) 5–6, 7–9, 15, 39, 45, 71,
  117–118
Churchill, Marigold (daughter) 29
Churchill, Mary (daughter; *later*
  Soames) 13, 29
Churchill, Randolph (son) 28,
  118, 134
Churchill, Sarah (daughter) 29
Churchill, Winston Spencer
  character and personality 2–5,
  8–11, 16–17, 19, 24–25, 73–74,
  89, 122–123
  chronology 125–129
  Conservative Party, defection
  and return 14, 16–18, 23–26, 37,
  41, 44
  depression 11–13, 40–41, 106
  early years 5–12, *10,* 125
  entry into politics 12–16, 125
  First Lord of the Admiralty 14,
  24, 32–33, 37, 61–62, *77,* 125, 127
  Freemasonry 72
  health 117–118, 126, 128, 129
  hobbies 126
  iconography of 73–74
  images of *4, 10, 40, 62,* 74, *78,*
  98, 112
  later years, death and state
  funeral 117–121, 129
  legacy and divisiveness 1–5,
  122–124
  marriage and children 27–29, 110
  military service 8–12, *10,* 14, 24,

32, 77, *78,* 125–126
as military strategist 77–85
anti-Nazi stance 52–61
in Opposition (1945-51)
104–114, 128
becoming Prime Minister, first
term 2–3, *4,* 61–70, *62,* 73–76,
104–107, 127
as Prime Minister, second term
114, 116–121, 128–129
political beliefs 13–16, 42–51
popularity 75–76, 104–105
racism 99–102
social reforms of 18–22
on Socialism 3, 20–21, 106–107
tanks, invention of 37–38
ten facts about 71–72
Tonypandy riots, role in 25–26,
125
vision for Anglo-American
union 85–94, 95–96, 103,
109–110, 119–120, 124
on votes for women 26–31
war memoirs 39, 65, 68, 70–71,
85, 97, 122
as "warmonger" 114–116
writings, novels and journalism
9–12, 109–110, 125, 129
see also Speeches
Cockran, Bourke 9
Collins, Michael 50–51
Communism 55, 95–96, 98–99,
128
Conservative Party
as Coalition 36–37, 42, 44
conferences, W.S.C. speeches
113–114, 118–119
general election 1945, loss
104–107
and Neville Chamberlain 57,
63–64, 68
and return to Gold Standard
46–47, 51
on votes for women 27–28
on W.S.C. as Prime Minister,
first term 62, 64–66, 68
W.S.C. defection and return 14,
16–18, 23–26, 37, 41, 44
and W.S.C. final government
116–121
on the Yalta agreement 101–102

Cooper, Duff 60–61
Cripps, Sir Stafford 73, 75
Cromwell, Oliver 63, 77
Cuba, W.S.C. in 9, 72
Czechoslovakia 58–59, 127

D
Daily Graphic 9
Daily Mirror 114
Dardanelles campaign 33–34, *34,*
39, 125
Dunkirk, evacuation of 66–68,
75, 127

E
Eden, Anthony 57–58, 85, 118,
120, 127
Edward VII, King 21
Edward VIII, King 56–57, 127
Edwards, Ralph 82–83
Eisenhower, Dwight D. 102–103,
111, 120, 128–129
Empire, British *see* British
Empire
Enigma codes 80–81
European unity, post-WWII
111–114, 128
Everest, Mrs (nanny) 6

F
Fisher, John "Jacky," 1st Baron
32, 36
Free Trade 14, 16–18, 46

G
Gallipoli campaign 32–41, *34,*
42–43, 125–126
Gandhi, Mahatma 56
Gardiner, A.G. 16
Garnett, Theresa 26–27
General Elections
pre-WWI 13–14, 21–22
inter-war years 42, 44, 49, 51,
62, 106
post-WWII 104–107, 114, 128
General Strike (1926) 48–50
George VI, King 65, 128
German cities, British bombing
84–85
Germany *see* Hitler, Adolf; Nazi
Germany; World War One

Gilbert, Martin 11–12, 134
Gold Standard, return to 45–51, 126
Greece 98–101, 127–128
Greenwood, Arthur 65, 67
Grigg, John 85–86

H
Halifax, Edward F.L. Wood, 1st Earl 62–65, 67–68
Harriman, Pamela (*née* Digby; *formerly* Churchill) 28
Harrow School 5, 6–8, 125
Hastings, Max 2–3, 84
Hitler, Adolf 52–61, 66–67, 86, 95, 126–128
Hume, David 115–116

I
India 11–12, 53, 100–102, 126
Ireland 14–15, 22, 49–51, 126
Ismay, Hastings, 1st Baron 79
Italy, in WWII 81–82, *93–94*

J
Jacob, Sir Ian 83
Japan, in WWII 58, 69, 82, 88, 127
Jenkins, Roy 116–117
Jews 46, 99–100
Jung, Carl 122–123

K
Kennedy, John F. 72
Keyes, Sir Roger 74–75
Keynes, John Maynard 47–48, 51
Kimball, Warren 88–89
Kitchener, Horatio Herbert, 1st Earl 35–36
Knight, Nigel 3–5

L
Labour Party 18, 21, 28, 43, 44, 104–108, 115, 128
on W.S.C. 23–24, 62, 63–65, 67,114
League of Nations 45–46, 55, 59
Liberal Party 27–28, 36, 42, 44, 65, 67
Liberalism, and 'New Liberalism' 18–19, 20, 23
Lippmann, Walter 110–111

Lloyd George, David
inter-war years 42, 44–46, 49–50, 126
and social reform 17–19, 21, 23, 46
and WWI 24, 32, 41, 126

M
MacDonald, James Ramsay 53
McEvoy, Ambrose
Winston Churchill portrait *40*
Macmillan, Harold 119
Macready, Gen. Sir Nevil, 1st Baronet 25–26
Masterman, Charles 19
Middle East 24, 45–46, 69, 80–82, 126, 127
Monckton, Walter 119
Montgomery, Bernard Law, 1st Viscount 75–76
Moran, 1st Baron (Charles McMoran Wilson) 12–13, 103
Morton, Desmond 90
Munich conference 59–61, 101, 127
Mussolini, Benito 57, 59, 127

N
Nation, The 47–48
National Theatre 71
Nazi Germany 52–65, 66–67, 69, 80–82, 95–97, 124, 127–128
map of occupied territory *93–94*
New York Times, The 110
Nicolson, Harold 58, 70
Niemeyer, Sir Otto 47–48
Norman, Montagu, 1st Baron
Norman 47, 51
Nuclear threat 116, 121

P
Poland, vulnerability in WWII 96–97, 100–102
Pound, Admiral Sir Dudley 79–80

R
Reade, Winwood 11
Rearmament 54–55, 57, 115, 126
Reynolds, David 87
Rhodes James, Robert 53
Roosevelt, Franklin D. 85–91, *98*, 102–103, 123–124, 126–128

Rosebery, Archibald Primrose, 5th Earl 15–16

S
Sackville-West, Vita 58
St Helier, Mary Jeune, Baroness 27
Sandhurst, The Royal Military Academy 6–8, 125
Scobie, Gen. Ronald 99–100
Singapore, British surrender 69, 82, 127
Skidelsky, Robert 47, 51
Socialism 3, 20–21, 106–107
Soviet Union
    Bolshevik/October Revolution 43–44
    in League of Nations 55, 59
    and WWII 69, 95–103, 120–121
    post-WWII 93–94, 104, 107–108, 116
Speeches
    80th birthday (1954) 75–76
    on Anglo-American union (1943) 90–93
    on appeasement (1938) 60
    on army reform (1901) 15
    in Bristol (1909) 26–29
    on European unity (1946) 111–114, 128
    first as Prime Minister (1940) 66
    on Gandhi (1931) 56
    to honour Ellen Terry (1906) 71
    to House of Commons (1916) 40
    to House of Commons (1942) 70
    "Iron Curtain" (1946) 107–110, 111, 128
    on Middle East (1921) 45
    on nuclear threat (1955) 121
    oratory skill 9, 17–18, 19, 70, 118–119, 123
    radio broadcasts 1, 62, 73–76, 95, 106
    on rearmament (1936) 54
    on Socialism (1908) 20
    on votes for women (1910) 30
    on Yalta agreement (1945) 101
Stalin, Joseph 93, 95–103, *98*, 120, 124, 127–128
Storr, Anthony 11, 122–123

Suez crisis 111, 120
Suffragette movement 26–31

T
Tanks, invention of 37–38
Taylor, A.J.P. 79
Terry, Ellen 71
Tonypandy riots 25–26, 125
Truman, Harry S. 102–103, 107, 108–109, 119–120, 128

U
United States
    Anglo-American union, W.S.C. vision for 85–94, 95–96, 103, 109–110, 119–120, 124
    Honorary Citizenship of W.S.C. 72, 129
    and WWII 85–94, *93–94*, 95–96, 124, 127

V
Versailles Treaty 58–59

W
Wardlaw-Milne, Sir John 74–75
Washington Post, The 110
Women, votes for 26–31
World War One 24, 30, 32–41, *34*, 42–43, 77–79, *78*, 125–126
World War Two
    and appeasement to Hitler 52–61
    chronology 126–127
    Soviet Union, and W.S.C.'s concessions to 95–103, *98*, 124
    U.S. involvement 85–94, *93–94*, 95–96, 124, 127
W.S.C. as war leader *4*, 61–70, *62*, 73–76, 77–85, *112*, 124
W.S.C. spirit *vs.* judgement 2–3, 62, 115, 122–124
W.S.C. war memoirs 39, 65, 68, 70–71, 85, 97, 122

Y
Yalta Conference, and the "Big Three" *98*, 100–103, 128

First published in 2016 by
Connell Guides
Artist House
35 Little Russell Street
London WC1A 2HH

10 9 8 7 6 5 4 3 2 1

Picture credits:
p.4 © Murray Sanders/REX/Shutterstock
p.40 © National Portrait Gallery, London
p.62 © MARKA / Alamy Stock Photo
p.78 © World History Archive / Alamy Stock Photo
p.93-94 © Connell Guides
p.98 © John Jochimsen/REX/Shuterstock
p.112 ©Everett/REX/Shuterstock

A CIP catalogue record for this book is available from the British Library.
ISBN 978-1-907776-84-7

Design © Nathan Burton
Written by Paul Addison
Edited by Jolyon Connell and Anna Neima

Assistant Editors and Typesetting by
Paul Woodward and Holly Bruce

www.connellguides.comm

How good a military strategist was he?   77
Did Churchill pay too high a price for
Britain's alliance with the US?   85
Did Churchill make too many
concessions to Stalin?   95

Post-war   **104**
Why did Churchill lose the general
election of 1945?   104
What was Churchill's post-war vision?   107
Was Churchill a warmonger?   114
What did his final government achieve?   116

Conclusion: The Churchill myth   **122**

NOTES

Churchill's 'black dog': fact or myth?   *11*
The Tonypandy affair   *25*
Marriage and children   *27*
Chuchill and the invention of the tank   *37*
Churchill and the Middle East   *45*
Churchill and Ireland   *49*
Ten facts about Winston Churchill   *71*
The iconography of Churchill   *73*
Was Churchill a racist?   *99*
Journalist and author   *109*
The state funeral   *117*
A short chronology   *125*
Endnotes   *129*
Further reading   *134*

Introduction

It is almost impossible to exaggerate just how famous Churchill was at the end of the Second World War. Most people around the world would have known his name, heard his voice on the radio or seen his face beaming or glowering in the newsreels. At home in Britain, but also more widely among the allied nations, he was acknowledged as a great war leader. Fame and glory, however, are highly perishable commodities. It was also unclear that the wartime legend of Churchill would survive the scrutiny of historians. At the time of his death in January 1965 surprisingly little was known of the inside story of his politics, his statesmanship or his private life. Except for what Churchill himself had written, the evidence lay hidden in the archives, most of which were closed.

With the opening of the archives a boom in Churchill studies began. Of all the politicians of 20th century Britain he is the only one to have inspired an apparently never-ending cascade of books, articles and docu-dramas. Part of the explanation lies in the fact that his place in our past is still in dispute. He is as controversial today as he was for much of his lifetime, and most of those who study him fall, broadly speaking, into one of two schools of thought: the pro- and the anti-Churchill. Neutrality and indifference are rare.

1

The pro-Churchill case rests on two main contentions. The first is that in the Second World War he was the saviour of his country and more generally of freedom in the western world. He came to power in May 1940 at a point where Britain was demoralised and almost defeated. But for his leadership and inspiration, the British might have given up the struggle and allowed Hitler to conquer the whole of Europe. If he made serious mistakes – and most of his admirers concede that he did – they pale into insignificance in comparison with the achievements. Hence the historian Geoffrey Best can write:

> In the years 1940 and 1941 he was indeed the saviour of the nation. His achievements, taken in all, justify his title to be known as the greatest Englishman of his age. I am persuaded that, in this later time, we are diminished if, admitting Churchill's failings and failures, we can no longer appreciate his virtues and victories. [1]

The second contention is that Churchill was an exceptional human being, a rare and brilliant creature of extraordinary energy and vision, literary and rhetorical flair, physical and moral courage, a man of genius who stood head and shoulders above his rivals.

As Max Hastings puts it, Churchill was "the largest human being ever to occupy his office". [2]

The anti-Churchill case starts from the proposition that he was more of a liability than an asset in World War Two. He inflicted great damage on the Empire, sacrificed the interests of Britain to those of the Soviet Union and the United States, and opened the door to socialism at home. His mistakes stemmed from overweening egotism, self-delusion and lack of strategic judgment, and his performance as a war leader was all of a piece with his earlier career, which had been littered with failures like the Gallipoli campaign of 1915. His legacy was the illusion that Britain had won the war and was still a great power when the reality was defeat and decline. The case is memorably summed up by John Charmley:

> Churchill stood for the British Empire, for British independence and for an "anti-Socialist" vision of Britain. By July 1945 the first of these was on the skids, the second was dependent solely on America and the third had just vanished in a Labour election victory.[3]

On this analysis, Churchill's heroic status is a skilfully propagated myth which it is incumbent on historians to demolish. It is no surprise that Churchill's detractors, with some exceptions, take a hostile view of his motives and qualities. One of his more recent biographers, Nigel Knight,

Opposite: A World War II poster

describes his personality as "a mixture of arrogance, emotion, self-indulgence, stubbornness and a blind faith in his own ability.".[4]

The early years

How did the young Churchill achieve so much so quickly?

Restless ambition was the main driving force in Churchill's life. From his schooldays at Harrow onwards his hunger for power and glory was transparent. At the age of 16 he confided to a fellow schoolboy that he sometimes dreamed of a future in which London would be in danger and it would fall to him, as the commander of the city's defences, to save the capital and the Empire. Already he saw himself as a Man of Destiny, intended to play a heroic role in his nation's history.

Churchill was born into an aristocracy which for centuries had supplied many of the nation's rulers. He was a direct descendant of John Churchill, the first duke of Marlborough, Queen Anne's victorious commander-in-chief during the War of the Spanish Succession. But it was above all his desire to emulate his father that inspired him to enter politics. Lord Randolph (1849-1895) was the impetuous third son of the seventh duke of

Marlborough. After a whirlwind courtship he married Jeanette Jerome (1854–1921), the daughter of a buccaneering New York financier, at the British Embassy in Paris on 15 April 1874. The date of Winston's birth – 30 November – has given rise to speculation that he was conceived before the wedding, but he may simply have been a premature baby.

Churchill had a turbulent and in some ways unhappy childhood. He adored his father and mother but demanded more attention from them than upper class parents of the time usually gave to their children. Lord Randolph's life was devoted mainly to politics: Winston could recall only two or three long and intimate conversations with him. Lady Randolph, meanwhile, revelled in high society. "She shone for me like the Evening Star," Churchill wrote. "I loved her dearly—but at a distance."[5] His nanny, Mrs Everest, supplied the love and admiration he craved and he responded with remarkably open displays of affection for his "Woom" or "Woomany". Churchill longed for his parents to visit him at school at Harrow. When they failed to do so he invited Mrs Everest instead and walked arm in arm with her up the High Street. During her final illness in July 1895 Churchill, by that time a Sandhurst cadet, rushed to her bedside, afterwards arranging the funeral and the erection of a gravestone.

Legend has it that Churchill was a dunce at

Harrow, but while absolutely refusing to learn Latin, which he detested, he demonstrated great ability in English, History, and Chemistry. As Gerald Woods Wollaston, a Harrow contemporary, recalled, "he resolutely refused to absorb anything that did not interest him".

He also displayed an aggressively delinquent streak. Woods Wollaston observed that he "consistently broke almost every rule made by masters or boys, was quite incorrigible, and had an unlimited vocabulary of 'back-chat', which he produced with dauntless courage on every occasion of remonstrance".[6] According to his cousin, Shane Leslie, he was deeply unpopular and had to be rescued by a master when a set of bullies pushed him head downwards into a fold-up bed into which they poured water. "Far from emerging penitent, Winston walked up and down orating in his wrath to the effect that one day he would be a great man when they were nobodies and he would stamp and crush them!"[7] He was not good at team games but shone at individual pursuits – he was a strong swimmer, excelled at rifle shooting, and won the public schools fencing championship in 1892.

None of this could appease his father when he twice failed the entrance exams for Sandhurst, passing in at the third attempt with marks too low to qualify him for the infantry. Lord Randolph threatened to break off all contact with his son and warned:

if you cannot prevent yourself from leading the idle useless unprofitable life you have had during your schooldays & later months you will become a mere social wastrel, one of the hundreds of the public school failures.[8]

At Sandhurst, where cadets were instructed in technical military topics like fortifications and tactics, Churchill was an eager and successful candidate, passing out 20th out of 130. His success, however, was overcast by the decline of Lord Randolph, who had risen to be Chancellor of the Exchequer in 1886 but resigned when the Cabinet and the Prime Minister rejected his proposals for cuts in the defence budget. He never held office again. As a cadet Churchill had begun to win his father's respect, but the relationship was nipped in the bud by Lord Randolph's death at the age of 45, on 24 January 1895.

This was a turning point. Churchill believed that his father's death, like that of his uncle, the eighth duke of Marlborough, "was yet further proof that the Churchills died young".[9] He was henceforth driven by the need to vindicate his father's reputation and to make his own mark before it was too late. He obtained his commission as a cavalry officer in the 4th Queen's Own Hussars. Much as he enjoyed soldiering, however, he saw it chiefly as a means to an end: the making of a reputation that would propel him into the

House of Commons. He longed to emulate his father. The journalist J.B. Atkins has described how

> when the prospects of a career like that of his father, Lord Randolph, excited him, then such a gleam shot from him that he was almost transfigured. I had not before encountered this type of ambition, unabashed, frankly egotistical, communicating its excitement, and extorting sympathy.[10]

Churchill's life is all too easily read as a tale of privilege, and his background certainly helps explain why he climbed so high at a comparatively young age. He was, nevertheless, a man of exceptional drive and outstanding ability. His physical courage was remarkable, his energy prodigious. At some point in the 1890s he began to realise his formidable skills as a writer and orator. Perhaps the critical year was 1895, when he undertook to write a series of dispatches from Cuba for the Daily Graphic, his first venture into journalism. It was also the year in which he met the Irish-American politician Bourke Cockran. More than half a century later he was still paying tribute to Cockran as the man who inspired his oratory and taught him how to use his voice: "He was my model. I learned from him how to hold thousands in thrall."[11]

Opposite: Wintston Churchill, the young cavalry officer, in 1895

In October 1896 Churchill sailed with his regiment to India. Quartered in the British military compound at Bangalore, with his ambitions fixed firmly on politics, he feared he would be handicapped by the lack of a University education. With the aid of books supplied by his mother, he turned himself into an autodidact, reading Plato, Adam Smith, Gibbon, Macaulay, Hallam, Lecky, Darwin, and Winwood Reade. The latter's *Martyrdom of Man*, a classic of Victorian atheism, completed his progressive loss of faith in Christianity and left him with a sombre vision of a godless universe in which humanity was destined, nevertheless, to progress through the conflict between the more advanced and the more backward races.

Churchill pursued a spectacular programme of self-advertisement between 1895 and 1900,

CHURCHILL'S 'BLACK DOG': FACT OR MYTH?

Some authorities maintain that Churchill suffered from severe and recurrent episodes of depression. The psychiatrist Anthony Storr, for example, has argued that Churchill fought a lifelong battle against despair. In his view Churchill's ability to raise the spirits of his fellow citizens in the dire circumstances of 1940 was rooted in his ability to vanquish his own "Black Dog".

Churchill's official biographer, Sir Martin Gilbert, while recognising that he was naturally downcast when things went wrong, could find no making his name and providing him with a platform for entry into politics. His strategy was to combine soldiering with authorship. With brash self-confidence and the assistance of his parents' contacts, he gate-crashed his way into battle, fighting Afghan tribesmen on the north-west frontier of India, the dervishes of the Sudan, and the Boers in South Africa. His escape from a Boer prisoner-of-war camp turned him briefly into a hero at home. Each time he managed to combine his military activities with working as a war correspondent. He expanded his dispatches into books: *The Story of the Malakand Field Force* (1898), *The River War* (2 vols, 1899), *London to Ladysmith* (1900) and *Ian Hamilton's March* (1900). He even found time to write a novel, *Savrola* (1900), a melodramatic tale of a liberal revolution in an autocratic Mediterranean state.

evidence of an inherent tendency to depression. Many of Churchill's admirers are equally inclined to dismiss the Black Dog as a myth. They see him as an embodiment of healthy, extrovert masculinity, and do not warm to the idea that he possessed a psychological weakness or flaw.

It is difficult to draw conclusions about Churchill's inner life from the scraps of evidence available. He does appear to have suffered a serious bout of depression at some point early in his career. He told his doctor, Lord Moran, that for two or three years "the light faded out of the picture. I did my work. I sat in the House of Commons, but black depression settled on me. It helped me to talk to Clemmie about it."[12] In July 1911 he wrote to Clemmie to

From MP to Cabinet minister

Did Churchill have a political ideology?

Churchill was first elected to the House of Commons as the Tory MP for Oldham in the general election of 1900. In 1904 he crossed the

say how interested he had been to hear of a German doctor who cured a cousin of depression: "I think this man might be quite useful to me – if my black dog returns. He seems quite away from me now – It is such a relief. All the colours came back into the picture. Brightest of all your dear face – my Darling."[13] This is the only direct reference we have by Churchill himself to his Black Dog, but according to his doctor, his daughter Mary and his intimate friend Brendan Bracken, he spoke of it as a familiar problem. Bracken told Moran: "Winston has been so successful in controlling his fears that most people think of him as restless. But he has

had to struggle with a fearful handicap... You see, Charles, Winston has always been a 'despairer'." [14]

It is possible that Churchill suffered as a young man from a phase of depression that lifted and did not return. There is, however, no evidence to show that he was permanently afflicted, and none to show that he was bipolar. After his death his private secretary, Jock Colville, asked his wife for her views on the subject. "She was quite positive," Colville wrote, "that although her husband was occasionally depressed – as indeed most normal people are – he was not abnormally subject to long fits of depression."[15] ∎

floor of the House over the question of free trade, and took his seat with the Liberals on the Opposition benches. The consequences of the decision for his career were immense. In the general election of 1906 a last great revival lifted the party into power and Churchill climbed rapidly to the top of British politics. The Prime Minister Campbell Bannerman gave him his first post as Under-Secretary at the Colonial Office (1905-8). On succeeding to the premiership in 1908 Herbert Asquith raised him to the Cabinet as President of the Board of Trade (1908-10), going on to appoint him as Home Secretary (1910-11) and First Lord of the Admiralty (1911-15).

This rapid ascent marked him out as a potential prime minister, but his change of party came at a price. Most Conservatives reviled him as a turncoat and when the opportunity for revenge eventually arose they struck hard, inflicting near fatal damage on his career. His change of party raised a question that was to haunt him for the rest of his political life: was he, whatever his abilities or achievements, anything more than a great opportunist?

Even before his entry into the House of Commons Churchill was something of a misfit in party politics. In April 1897, while a 22-year-old subaltern in Bangalore, he wrote to Lady Randolph:

I am a Liberal in all but name. My views excite the pious horror of the Mess. Were it not for

Home Rule [for Ireland] – to which I would never consent – I would enter Parliament as a Liberal. As it is, Tory Democracy will have to be the standard under which I shall range myself.[16]

As a backbench Tory MP, Churchill found himself in sympathy with the Liberal Opposition on a number of points, such as the need to offer generous peace terms to the Boers. In his second major speech in the House, in May 1901, he summoned up the ghost of his father in a root-and-branch attack on the proposals of the Secretary for War, Sir John Brodrick, for army reform. Lord Randolph, he argued, had sacrificed his career in the cause of economy in public spending and opposition to militarism – again, strongly Liberal sentiments.

In July 1902 Arthur Balfour succeeded his uncle Lord Salisbury as Prime Minister. If Balfour had invited Churchill into the government, he would surely have leapt at the chance and bound himself to the Tories (at least for the time being). Balfour, however, remained aloof, and Churchill looked instead to the former Liberal Prime Minister, Lord Rosebery, to whom he wrote in October 1902, speculating on the possibility of a realignment of the parties:

The Government of the Middle – the party wh[ich] shall be free at once from the sordid selfishness and callousness of Toryism on the one hand, and the blind appetites of the Radical masses on the other – may be an ideal wh[ich] we perhaps shall never attain, wh[ich] could in any case only be possessed for a short time, but which is nevertheless worth working for; and I, for my part, see no reason to despair of that "good state".[17]

This takes us closer to the nature of Churchill's politics. He was attracted to both Tory and Liberal personalities and policies, and frequently in favour of some form of coalition. He could play the party game with a will, and relish the fight, but what he really believed in was strong, pragmatic rule by a Cabinet free from party doctrine.

In his own mind Churchill was an independent statesman whose mission was to lead parties, not follow them. As one of his contemporaries, the journalist A.G. Gardiner, put it: "To his imperious spirit a party is only an instrument. *Au fond* he would no more think of consulting a party than the chauffeur would think of consulting the motor car."[18]

Why did he abandon the Tory party?

In May 1903 the Colonial Secretary, Joseph Chamberlain, broke with the historic consensus in favour of free trade and proclaimed his conversion to protectionism ("tariff reform"). The Tories were split asunder. Churchill, who had been schooled in orthodox economics by the Permanent Secretary to the Treasury, Francis Mowatt, leapt into the fray on behalf of the Tory free traders. He expected them to win the battle for control of the party, but within a few months they were all but crushed by the protectionists, who succeeded in capturing Churchill's own constituency party in Oldham. As he refused to recant, the Oldham activists withdrew their support. The notion that he abandoned his party is misleading; it would be nearer the truth to say that he was driven out.

Free trade was one of the prime articles of faith of the Liberal party and the Liberals were eager to embrace him. On the afternoon of 31 May 1904 he took his seat next to David Lloyd George on the Opposition benches. The Tories accused him of betraying his party out of naked self-interest. He was indeed transparently on the make, but on the question of free trade his ambitions were broadly in step with his convictions and his egotism decently clothed in public purpose.

The defection of this dashing young man with a famous Tory name was a gift to Liberal publicists. In the prolonged interval between the decline of the government and its fall (1904–6) he proved to be one of the great platform orators of the day, drawing the crowds with speeches in which he abused his former party with barbed wit and gleeful invective. By November 1904 nearly 200 Liberal constituency associations had invited him to speak. His appointment by Campbell Bannerman as Colonial Under-Secretary was a well-deserved reward for services rendered.

What did he achieve as a social reformer?

By 1906 MPs from all the major parties – Tories, Liberals and Labour (which had 29 MPs in the new Parliament) – were under pressure to show how they would reduce poverty and unemployment. The Tories argued for protectionism and Labour for socialist measures. When he first joined the Liberals Churchill was an exponent of the classic principles of *laissez-faire*. In company with others such as the "Welsh wizard" David Lloyd George (who, with his legendary charm and electrifying oratory, had an influence over Churchill no one else ever matched), he now began to embrace the 'New Liberalism', a version of collectivism in which a measure of state intervention was combined with a continuing commitment to free trade, competitive capitalism, and the liberty of the individual.

When Churchill arrived at the Board of Trade in April 1908, he found himself in charge of a department whose expertise in the workings of the labour market would give him the opportunity of pursuing his new idea. The alliance he formed with Lloyd George, the Chancellor of the Exchequer, and the support they both received from Asquith, established the ascendancy of the New Liberalism over the old.[19]

Churchill's enthusiasm for social reform was intense and illustrated the extraordinary fashion in which his mind worked. He was renowned in Cabinet for monologues in which it was uncertain whether he was the master of the words that poured from his lips, or they the master of him. The Liberal Charles Masterman, who worked closely with him, observed:

> In nearly every case an idea enters his head from the outside. It then rolls round the hollow of his brain, collecting strength like a snowball. Then, after whirling winds of rhetoric, he becomes convinced that it is right, and denounces everyone who criticises it. He is in the Greek sense a Rhetorician, the slave of the words which his mind forms about ideas. He sets ideas to Rhetoric as musicians set theirs to music. And he can convince himself of almost every truth if it is once allowed thus to start on its wild career through his rhetorical machinery.[20]

Churchill's vision of social reform was too wide-ranging and ambitious for the times, but he managed to introduce a <u>first instalment</u> of it. He was personally responsible for three important initiatives: <u>statutory minimum wages</u> in the "sweated trades" such as <u>tailoring, labour exchanges,</u> and <u>compulsory unemployment insurance</u> for workers in occupations with a particularly high risk of unemployment. Churchill thought of himself as a <u>humane paternalist</u>, broadening the basis of the social order through the creation by the state of a "<u>national minimum</u>" standard of living. His sympathy for the poor was genuine but his reforms, modelled on those of Bismarckian

ON SOCIALISM

"Socialism seeks to pull down wealth; Liberalism seeks to raise up poverty. Socialism would destroy private interests. Liberalism would preserve private interests in the only way in which they can safely and justly be preserved, namely by reconciling them with public right. Socialism would kill enterprise; Liberalism would rescue enterprise from the trammels of privilege and preference. Socialism assaults the pre-eminence of the individuals; Liberalism seeks, and shall seek more in the future, to build up a minimum standard for the mass. Socialism exalts the rule; Liberalism exalts the man. Socialism attacks capital; Liberalism attacks monopoly."

Kinnaird Hall, Dundee, 4 May 1908

Germany, were intended to stifle socialism, which he described as "a monstrous and imbecile conception which can find no real foothold in the brains and hearts of sensible people".[21]

Lloyd George was the real firebrand. In the "People's Budget" of 1909 he proposed a range of new taxes on wealth and landed property that enraged the Tory Party and prompted the House of Lords, which had a large Tory majority, to take the unprecedented step of rejecting the budget. Taking up the cry of "the Peers versus the People", Lloyd George and Churchill denounced the Lords at public meetings up and down the country. As an aristocrat Churchill was accused of betraying his class. As a party politician, however, he plunged into battle and rejoiced in the fray.

The outcome was less than a triumph for the Liberals. In the general election of January 1910 they won only 275 seats compared with 401 in 1906, and the Tories achieved a higher percentage of the vote. With the support of Labour and the Irish Nationalists, the two minority parties, the government could still be sure of a clear working majority, but at the cost of dependence on others. Following the death of King Edward VII in May 1910, Lloyd George made a dramatic bid to break the party political deadlock with a proposal for a grand coalition of Liberals and Tories. The party system, he argued, played into the hands of extremists: a coalition would free both parties from their extremists and open the way to compromise. Churchill was strongly in favour and very disappointed when the project collapsed and party warfare resumed. A second general election in December 1910 left the composition of the House of Commons virtually unchanged and eventually compelled the Tories to accept a reduction in the power of the Lords. With the issue resolved, Churchill hoped that the two main parties could now work together in greater harmony.

It was wishful thinking. Curtailing the veto power of the House of Lords removed the main constitutional obstacle to the passage of an Irish Home Rule bill, a measure to which the Tories were viscerally opposed. Between 1911 and 1914 party politics were so embittered by the Irish question that Liberals and Tories found themselves on opposite sides on the brink of an Irish civil war. As a leading member of the government Churchill was drawn into the conflict. The blows he landed on the Tories rubbed salt into wounds already inflamed by his defection and attacks on his former party. Bonar Law, who succeeded Balfour as leader of the Tory party in November 1911, was a puritanical Scot who detested Irish Home Rule and was ready to support an armed revolt against it by the Protestants of Ulster. Churchill was a figure he viewed with deep mistrust.

Why did Churchill move back to the right?

The New Liberalism was predicated on a progressive alliance in which the Liberals were the dominant force and Labour a junior partner. Churchill, however, had now changed course and set his sights on the goal of a coalition of moderate Liberals and Conservatives. He was not abandoning the reforms that he and Lloyd George had introduced, but opposing the development of Liberalism in a more radical direction.

Why the shift? The evidence is patchy but we are free to speculate. Churchill's tenure of the Home Office coincided with a wave of industrial unrest accompanied, on the part of some trade unionists, by talk of direct action and a general strike. This is likely to have nudged Churchill to the right. When a national rail strike began in August 1911 he overrode the local authorities and despatched troops to many parts of the country to safeguard installations. When rioters attempted to prevent the movement of a train at Llanelli in Wales, troops opened fire and shot two men dead. In a pamphlet entitled 'Killing No Murder' the Labour leader Keir Hardie accused Churchill and Asquith of deliberately employing troops to kill strikers. Churchill became a Labour bête noire and Labour's mistrust of him was reciprocated by his

dislike him

hostility to trade union militancy.

At the same time he was waking up to the threat of war with Germany. From 1904 to 1910 he had argued that talk of an impending conflict was alarmist. The Home Office, however, brought him into contact with the newly formed Counter-Espionage Bureau run by Vernon Kell – the forerunner of MI5. Kell's belief that Germany had planted a network of agents and spies in Britain in preparation for war seems to have convinced him, and Churchill gave the Bureau strong support in collecting intelligence. From this it was but a short step to the conclusion that preparations for war were now the most urgent task, with the Tories more likely to assist than Labour or the Liberal Left.

In 1911 Churchill made a key intervention during a meeting of the Committee of Imperial Defence – called to discuss the brinkmanship between France and Germany in Agadir – and Asquith was persuaded to move him to the Admiralty. Churchill sensed destiny drawing near. Motoring down to Brighton with Lloyd George one weekend, he began to prophesy the course of the coming war. He described how he himself would be in command of the army, winning a decisive victory in the Middle East and returning to Britain in triumph. "And where do I come in?" Lloyd George enquired.[22]

Churchill's egotism was colossal and his pre-war career in politics marked by spectacular

U-turns. Nevertheless the Tory charge – that he was a political mercenary interested only in his own career – was too harsh. Churchill was never a partisan ideologue or loyalist. To assume that he should have been, and therefore failed to live up to the requisite standards, is to adopt a belief in political parties that he did not share, and historians are under no obligation to subscribe to. Mavericks deserve to be judged on their merits. Nor should the fact that Churchill changed course on a number of occasions be confused with the notion that he was a calculating opportunist. He thought he knew best and his political instability

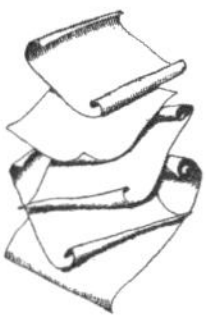

THE TONYPANDY AFFAIR

As Home Secretary, Churchill has often been accused of sending troops to shoot down striking Welsh miners at Tonypandy in November 1910, but this is not supported by the evidence. The only rioter killed was injured in a struggle with the Glamorgan police before Churchill intervened. The local magistrates then pleaded with the Home Office to send troops. Recognising that this might result in bloodshed, Churchill at first sent a detachment of the Metropolitan Police instead. Twenty-four hours later, when it was clear that the riots were continuing unabated, he authorised the despatch of troops.

In a bold and imaginative stroke (which may have been unconstitutional), he appointed General Neville Macready to command both troops and police, with instructions to ensure that the

[handwritten margin notes: "blindly follows the party", "independent"]

was due partly to the intuitive and imaginative nature of his mental processes, which swept him rapidly along from one position to another with barely a pause for thought.

What did Churchill think about votes for women?

On 13 November 1909 Churchill travelled by train to Bristol, where he was due to make a speech. He had just stepped down on to the platform when he was approached by Theresa Garnett, a suffragette,

police acted as a buffer between the strikers and the troops. In all probability this prevented further bloodshed – a conclusion supported by the evidence of one of the most prominent of the strikers, Will Mainwaring. Of Churchill's decision to send troops into the Rhondda in 1910 he said:

We never thought that Winston Churchill had exceeded his natural responsibility as Home Secretary. The military that came into the area did not commit one single act that allows the slightest

resentment by the strikers. On the contrary, we regarded the military as having come in the form of friends to modify the otherwise ruthless attitude of the police forces.[23]

In addition, the riots broke out on the eve of a general election, and the miners were mostly Liberal voters, so it would have been the height of folly for Churchill to employ the military against them. Nonetheless, following Tonypandy and the events at Llanelli, Churchill was routinely stereotyped as a hot-headed class warrior. ∎

who struck him over the head with a dog-whip. "Take that in the name of the insulted women of England!" she cried.[24] For a few seconds they grappled near the edge of the platform, almost in the path of a moving train, before Clementine jumped over a pile of luggage and pulled him back.

Churchill was not the only Cabinet minister harassed by the suffragettes. The majority of Liberals were – in principle – favourable to the enfranchisement of women, while most Conservatives were against, but it was the Liberals who were in power and refusing to act. Asquith, the Prime Minister, was opposed to the idea, though

MARRIAGE AND CHILDREN

In March 1908, shortly after joining the Cabinet, Churchill was invited to dinner by Lady St Helier. Seated on his right was Clementine Hozier (1885-1977) who was 23, beautiful, intelligent, an earnest Liberal and a supporter of votes for women. Churchill was captivated and they were married on 12 September 1908. Churchill expected his wife to be a loyal follower. The unhappy child of a disastrous and financially precarious marriage, she was contented with the role; she had found a monogamous and affectionate, if probably self-centred husband of whose statesmanship she was proud. She was, however, always one of his more critical admirers. A lifelong Liberal with a puritan streak, she never approved of Churchill's more louche Tory companions such as F.E. Smith (Lord Birkenhead) or Max Aitken, (Lord this was not the only reason for Liberal indecision. To give the vote to women on the same terms as men would be to enfranchise female householders, who in the main were affluent and likely to vote Tory. If, on the other hand, the Liberals scrapped the household qualification in favour of universal suffrage, they would be extending the vote to millions of working class women, many of whom might vote Labour.

Although he was on record as a supporter of votes for women, Churchill shared these anxieties. In addition, he bitterly resented suffragette attempts to disrupt his speeches and refused to be

Beaverbrook). She also often gave him sound political advice, which he seldom took. They sometimes quarrelled furiously. Nevertheless they were quick to make up after a row, and their marriage was sustained by a lifelong mutual affection; Winston was always "Pug" or "Pig", Clementine "Kat", and the children "the Kittens".

Winston and Clementine had five children. Diana (1909-1963) was twice married and divorced and committed suicide. Randolph (1911-1968) was a successful journalist but embarrassed his father with his boorishness, heavy drinking, and tactless interventions in politics. "We have a deep animal love for one another," Winston said, "but every time we meet we have a bloody row."[25] In 1939 Randolph married Pamela Digby and they had a son, Winston, born during the Blitz.

Subsequently Pamela embarked on an affair with Roosevelt's special emissary, Averell Harriman. Towards the end of his life Churchill agreed that Randolph should write his official biography, of which he had completed the first two volumes before he died.

"hen-pecked" into changing his position. In return, the suffragettes had grounds for resenting him. His appointment as Home Secretary in January 1910 coincided with an uneasy truce between the government and the suffragettes. Churchill rejected their plea to be classified as prisoners of conscience rather than common prisoners, though he did announce a relaxation of prison discipline. If, however, they went on hunger strike they were to lose their privileges and would also be subjected to forcible feeding. This was a horrifying practice which Churchill's friend W.S. Blunt likened to torture, but the Cabinet refused to allow the women to starve themselves to death and Churchill was all in favour of the policy.

The third child, Sarah (1914-1982), trained as a dancer and married, to the horror of her parents, the Austrian comedian Vic Oliver. He had already been married twice and his third marriage proved to be short-lived. Sarah then joined the Women's Auxiliary Air Force before resuming her career in theatre and film after the war.

The death at the age of three of their fourth child, Marigold (1918-1921) was a savage blow from which Winston and Clementine found some consolation in the birth the following year of Mary (1922-2015). The most well-balanced of the children, she joined the Auxiliary Territorial Service during the war, served in anti-aircraft batteries, and accompanied her father to the Quebec Conference of 1943. She married the diplomat Christopher Soames, worked hard and successfully to sustain her father's memory, and wrote a definitive life of her mother. ∎

The suffragettes laid two other offences at Churchill's door. In the spring of 1910 he appeared to promise that he would support a franchise bill to give the vote to women householders. When the bill was debated in the House, on 12 July 1910, however, he attacked it root and branch. "It would be possible," he declared, "for a woman to have a vote while living in a state of prostitution, if she married and became an honest woman she would lose that vote, but she would regain it through divorce."[26] This was unforgiveable: not only a betrayal on Churchill's part but a very well-argued one.

When the bill ran out of parliamentary time in November, the truce between the government and the suffragettes came to an end, and a deputation of 300 suffragettes laid siege to the House of Commons in protest. The brutal handling of the women by the metropolitan police led the suffragettes to call this "Black Friday" (18 November 1910). Since the Home Secretary was responsible for the metropolitan police, they assumed, quite mistakenly, that Churchill had given instructions for rough handling. Churchill was innocent of the charge but determined to protect the police by refusing an enquiry, which only lent colour to their suspicions.

On the eve of the First World War the suffragettes and the government were locked in stalemate, but the war quickly led to a truce. The government released the imprisoned suffragettes, most of whom agreed to co-operate in the recruitment of men to the army. The antagonism with Churchill dissolved, and he voted in favour of the Representation of the People Act (1918), which extended the franchise to all men over the age of 21 and women over the age of 30, still ensuring that the majority of the electorate was male.

Churchill admired beauty in women, had a handful of close female friends, and loved to be pampered and spoilt by society hostesses, but what women were doing in the masculine realm of politics he never quite understood. The first woman to take her seat in the Commons was Nancy Astor, whose presence there Churchill plainly resented. When she asked him why he behaved so rudely to her he replied: "Because I find a woman's intrusion into the House of Commons as embarrassing as if she burst into my bathroom when I had nothing with which to defend myself, not even a sponge."[25]

The First World War

Was Churchill to blame for Gallipoli?

Once at the Admiralty the dynamism Churchill had displayed in social reform was redirected towards the reorganisation of the Royal Navy. It was far from certain that a war with Germany was inevitable but this was the contingency for which he began to prepare. Encouraged by the (then retired) First Sea Lord, "Jackie" Fisher, the father of the Dreadnought and most celebrated British sailor of his day, Churchill converted the Fleet from coal to oil, ordered the construction of the new 15-inch gun class of battleship, pressed ahead with the building of submarines and set up the Royal Naval Air Service. His determination to ensure that Britain remained ahead in the great naval race with Germany led to a Cabinet crisis in January 1914 when he demanded a big increase in the naval budget which was opposed by Lloyd George. Churchill got the better of the argument. The last few days of peace found him among the hawks rather than the doves in the Cabinet. On 1 August 1914, acting without the authorisation of the Cabinet but with the tacit approval of Asquith, he ordered the Fleet to its war stations.

In the opening days of the war Churchill's

reputation stood high as the man who had made sure the Fleet was ready, but the Gallipoli campaign of 1915 proved to be a great military disaster and all but destroyed his reputation. In a futile attempt to knock Turkey out of the war, 132,000 British, French, Australian, New Zealand and Indian troops were killed or injured in conditions as hellish as anything on the Western Front. Most of the blame fell on Churchill, who was dismissed from the Admiralty. In the years between the two World Wars his detractors never ceased to taunt him with the cry of "Gallipoli". Churchill, however, always had a handful of loyal defenders who argued that he was made into a scapegoat for the mistakes of others and the inadequacy of the machinery for strategic decision-making.

At the outbreak of war the Royal Navy had two major strategic roles. The first was to maintain the supremacy of the British Fleet over the German High Seas Fleet in the North Sea, thus protecting Britain from invasion. The second was to enforce a long-range blockade of Germany. In November, however, Turkey had declared war on Britain. With stalemate on the Western Front the War Council took up the idea of a naval assault on the Gallipoli peninsular. The plan was to send a force of old battleships, surplus to requirements in the North Sea, to bombard the forts guarding the entrance to the Dardanelles, the narrow, 40-mile

Map of the Dardanelles area of the Gallipoli campaign, 1915-1916

long Straits leading from the Mediterranean to the Sea of Marmora. Once through the Straits the ships would appear off Constantinople, the Turkish capital, and the threat of a naval bombardment would compel Turkey to surrender. This would open up a warm water route through which supplies could be sent to assist the Russians on the eastern front, and might persuade some of the Balkan states to enter the war on the allied side.

Churchill was enthusiastic but his own priority at this stage was the capture of the island of Borkum on the north-west coast of Germany, to be

34

followed by the establishment of naval supremacy in the Baltic. He adopted a naval assault on Gallipoli, however, as a minor, low-risk operation that would provide an "interlude" while he pressed ahead with plans for Borkum.

Initially, Churchill argued that Gallipoli should take the form of a combined operation employing troops to occupy the heights and safeguard the passage of warships through the Straits. If a combined operation along these lines had been properly planned, it might have succeeded. Lord Kitchener, the Secretary for War, however, was reluctant to release troops from the Western Front and Churchill convinced himself, on the basis of rather equivocal evidence from his naval advisers, that the Straits could be forced by ships alone. The War Council, meanwhile, had decided that "boots on the ground" might, as Churchill had originally argued, prove essential. Instead of cancelling the purely naval assault, however, they authorised Churchill to go ahead with it on 19 February.

At first all went well. An Anglo-French flotilla of 16 ships bombarded the outer forts of the peninsular and entered the Straits. Churchill was euphoric. But the progress of the warships was impeded by minefields and crossfire from Turkish forts on both sides of the Straits, and, to Churchill's great frustration, the naval attack was halted while troops assembled in the eastern Mediterranean for a combined assault.

In a rational world there would have been no resumption of the naval offensive until the troops were in place for a combined assault. But Churchill and the War Council had invested too much political capital in the operation to admit that it had failed, and the naval offensive was resumed – until the loss of three battleships, sunk by mines, convinced the naval commander in the Straits to call a halt once more. Furious but impotent, Churchill was compelled to await the fate of the troops who landed on Gallipoli on 25 April.

Operations on land were the responsibility of Kitchener and Sir Ian Hamilton, the commander of the Allied Expeditionary Force. As the landings turned into a stalemate, leaving the troops stranded on narrow strips of beach under fire from the Turks on the heights above them, Churchill was little more than a spectator. In an attempt to overcome the stalemate he again demanded a renewal of the naval assault, a move that that led to his downfall. Fisher, the First Sea Lord, was a revered national figure. To an extent that Churchill failed to appreciate, he had become an opponent of the naval operation, which he feared would divert resources from the North Sea. On 15 May 1915 he resigned, exposing Churchill to withering attack from his enemies in the Conservative Party. Unfortunately for Churchill, Fisher's resignation coincided with a munitions crisis that prompted Asquith to invite the Conservatives into a Coalition government.

The Conservatives, who <u>mistrusted</u> Churchill's interventions in <u>military</u> affairs, and had <u>never forgiven</u> him for his change of party, insisted that he be <u>dropped</u> from the <u>Admiralty</u>. Churchill was relegated to <u>minor office</u> and remained for the time being a <u>member</u> of the <u>Cabinet</u> committee in charge of the Gallipoli campaign. Stunned by his downfall and consumed by frustration, he urged <u>fresh attacks</u> but his <u>advice</u> was <u>ignored</u> and when the <u>committee</u> was <u>reformed</u> without him he <u>resigned</u>. In <u>December</u> the <u>War Council</u> decided to <u>admit defeat</u> and <u>evacuate Gallipoli</u>.

How far was Churchill to blame? For many

CHURCHILL AND THE INVENTION OF THE TANK

Churchill was fascinated by the application of science and technology to warfare and played an important role in the creation of the tank. A Royal Commission after the war concluded that "it was primarily due to the receptivity, courage and driving force of the Rt. Hon. Winston Spencer Churchill that the general idea of the use of such an instrument of warfare as the 'Tank' was converted into a practical shape".[28]

As deadlock set in on the Western Front towards the end of 1914, the military experts began to search for a way to restore a war of movement. In January 1915 Lieutenant Colonel Ernest Swinton presented the War Office with an ingenious plan for a "machine gun destroyer", an armour-plated vehicle with ten men inside, mounted on caterpillars and armed with machine guns. With its crew shielded from enemy fire, the years after 1915 the case against him was greatly exaggerated for reasons that were as much political as historical. Gallipoli was in large part a collective failure. The British were used to fighting minor colonial wars. The War Council was amateurish and failed to ensure joint planning by the War Office and the Admiralty. And it mistakenly assumed that the Turks were a backward race incapable of organising an effective defence. What was intended as a minor military operation fell victim to "mission creep" and turned into a major fiasco.

As the politician responsible for the initial naval

machine would advance at a speed of four miles an hour to capture the German trenches. Both Churchill and Maurice Hankey, the Secretary to the War Council, were much taken with the idea and persuaded the War Office to give it a trial. When the prototype machine fell into a trench and could not get out the War Office abandoned the experiment, but Churchill, meanwhile, was pursuing an alternative plan – for a 1,000-ton armoured vehicle to transport infantrymen. Although land warfare was the province of the War Office, Churchill made it sound like Admiralty business by the simple expedient of calling the new vehicle a "landship" and appointing an Admiralty Land Ship Committee to develop the project. Without the approval of the Board of Admiralty, the War Office, or the Treasury, he authorised the expenditure of £70,000 on the construction of 18 prototypes. The project was given the code name "water tank for Mesopotamia", from which the name "tank" derived. After initial trials it made its successful debut on the Somme on 15 September 1916. ∎

assault, Churchill rushed into it with too little preparation. He ignored the reservations about the operation expressed by his advisers at the Admiralty and failed to notify the War Council of their doubts. Like his father before him, he overestimated his own power, failed to understand how little he was trusted, and overplayed his hand. He had little if any responsibility for the later stages of the campaign but having been cast as the scapegoat for its early failures he became more desperate than ever for it to succeed in the end. When it didn't he was devastated. He was not to know that Gallipoli had taught him a lesson that would stand him in good stead between 1940 and 1945: never overrule your military advisers.

A fundamental question about Gallipoli remains. Was it a brilliant strategic concept, bungled in the execution, or an idea so flawed from the start that it could never have worked? Churchill's view was emphatic and never changed. In his memoirs of the Second World War he wrote: "I was ruined for the time being in 1915 over the Dardanelles, and a supreme enterprise was cast away, through my trying to carry out a major and cardinal operation of war from a subordinate position."[29] It is far from certain, however, that the defeat of the Ottoman Empire would have enabled the Allies to strike a decisive blow against the Kaiser.

After his resignation in November 1915 he sought active service on the front and was given

Sir Winston Leonard Spencer Churchill *by Ambrose McEvoy, circa 1915*

command of the 6th battalion of Royal Scots Fusiliers at Ploegsteert in Belgium. Lt. Col. Churchill proved a good commanding officer, combining inspiring leadership with great solicitude for the welfare of the ordinary soldier. The sector of the front on which he served was relatively quiet but he was often under fire and narrowly escaped death on a number of occasions. After four months at the front, however, he could no longer endure the frustration of exclusion from politics. He returned home in May 1916.

Back making speeches in the Commons, he was an isolated figure and prone to moods of despair.

When Asquith was succeeded by Lloyd George in December 1916 there was at first no place for Churchill. As Lloyd George knew, however, Churchill was a politician of outstanding ability who could be more dangerous in opposition than in office, and in July 1917 he brought him back into the government as Minister of Munitions. Although the post was one outside the War Cabinet, nearly 100 Conservative MPs signed a motion deploring the appointment. They believed that, for all his ability, there was "a tragic flaw in the metal". Lloyd George took a more generous view, arguing that Churchill could be useful as the member of a government in which "his more erratic impulses" were kept under control. "Men of his ardent temperament and powerful mentality need exceptionally strong brakes."[30]

The interwar years

How did Churchill's world-view change after World War One?

In the first post-war general election the Liberals were fatally split between a faction led by Asquith, which held aloof from the Coalition government, and a faction led by Lloyd George which opted to maintain the Coalition and fight the election in alliance with the Conservatives. The Coalition won a crushing victory in the course of which Churchill was re-elected in Dundee as a Lloyd George Liberal, and subsequently appointed by Lloyd George as Secretary for War and Air (1919-21) and Colonial Secretary (1921-2). He was now dependent on the personal patronage of the "Welsh wizard", while the wizard himself depended upon the support of the Conservative majority in the House of Commons.

Although Churchill remained a Liberal he was moving rapidly to the right. Before Gallipoli his politics had generally been the politics of optimism. Britain might have its troubles in Ireland, and the wave of strikes before World War One was alarming, but the British Empire was the greatest power on earth and Britain itself a land of social and economic progress. After Gallipoli, his world-view was overcast with pessimism. Destiny, it seemed, had abandoned him. In the aftermath of the war he was dismayed by the outbreak of nationalist revolts against British rule in Ireland, Egypt and India. The rise of Labour as a major party, and the growing support in the trade union world for a general strike, made him fearful of attacks on the social order at home.

Overshadowing all else in this darkening world-view was the Bolshevik revolution of 1917 in Russia, which he feared was at the bottom of all these disturbances. "Of all the tyrannies in history," he declared in April 1919, "the Bolshevik tyranny is the worst, the most destructive, and the most degrading. It is sheer humbug to pretend that it is not far worse than German militarism."[31]

The Bolshevik revolution resulted in a civil war between the Bolsheviks, who made peace with Germany, and the white armies of Generals Kolchak and Denikin. In 1918 the Allied powers sent troops and supplies to aid the white armies with the aim of bringing Russia back into the war, a decision in which Churchill took no part. The defeat of Germany, therefore, removed the primary purpose of Allied intervention. Churchill, now Secretary for War, was accordingly instructed by the War Cabinet to withdraw the 14,000 British troops stationed in Germany. He agreed, but tried almost at once to reverse the policy by urging the Supreme Allied War Council in Paris to send more troops to support the white Russian armies. He failed – defeated, in the end, partly by Lloyd George and partly by the failure of the white Russian armies – but his reputation as a hammer of the Bolsheviks lived on and helped rehabilitate him with the Conservatives.

Over the next few years Churchill's fortunes ebbed and flowed. When the Conservatives rebelled against the Coalition and brought down Lloyd George in October 1922, he, too, was thrown out of office. In the subsequent general election he lost his seat at Dundee.

He fought back with an astonishing display of political acrobatics, standing for the last time as a Liberal, at West Leicester, in the election of December 1923, and then, when the new House of Commons met, and the Liberals decided to support a minority Labour government, seizing the opportunity to break with them, only to reappear as an "Independent Anti-Socialist" at the Westminster (Abbey) by-election in March 1924. It was a blatant job application addressed to Conservative Central Office. He was then adopted as the "Constitutionalist" (i.e. Conservative) candidate for Epping, and returned to Parliament in the general election in October.

The Conservative Party was now his natural home, and had been since the First World War, but just as he had once been more radical than many of his fellow Liberals, now he became more extreme than many of his fellow Conservatives, a diehard defender of the world of his youth.

How much of a blunder was the return to the gold standard?

Having worked his passage back to the Conservatives, Churchill was delighted and surprised when Stanley Baldwin invited him to join his newly elected government as Chancellor of the Exchequer. He could now proudly wear his father's robes as Chancellor, stored away since 1887. This was a handsome reward for his

CHURCHILL AND THE MIDDLE EAST

In the aftermath of the First World War the pressures to reduce public spending were overwhelming. At the War Office, Churchill himself chafed at the expense involved in the British occupation of the former Ottoman territories of Palestine and Mesopotamia (Iraq) – regions which, he told the House of Commons in July 1921, were "unduly stocked with peppery, pugnacious, proud politicians and theologians".[32] He recommended that the League of Nations' mandate for Palestine be given to the United States: it was Lloyd George who insisted that it should go to Britain.

Churchill's drive for a settlement of the Middle East led him to propose that both Palestine and Iraq should be run by a new Middle East department of the Colonial Office. In February 1921, Lloyd George took the logical step of appointing him Colonial Secretary, and the new Middle East department was established, with a staff including T. E. Lawrence. In March Churchill visited Cairo to preside over a conference to settle the affairs of Palestine and Mesopotamia.

defection from the Liberals, though it was understood that he would maintain in all essentials the great Liberal cause of free trade. It also separated him from the politician Baldwin feared most: Lloyd George. Economics were, however, not his forte and his performance at the Treasury has never been highly rated. Nevertheless, he did please the Conservatives, the Treasury, and the Bank of England with his first major decision: in the budget of April 1925 he announced the

---

Although the details of the settlement owed much to others, it was Churchill who took the final decisions. Mesopotamia was transformed into the Kingdom of Iraq and the emir Feisal of the Hashemite dynasty was installed as the first monarch. To the dismay of Zionists, Churchill also decided that the whole of Palestine east of the River Jordan should become a second Arab kingdom of Transjordan under Feisal's brother, the emir Abdullah.

In accordance with the Balfour declaration of 1917, the League of Nations' mandate for Palestine included the provision that Palestine should become a "national home" for the Jews.

Under Churchill's settlement, the promise of a Jewish national home was to apply only to Palestine west of the Jordan, and even then it was to be cautiously interpreted.

Though Churchill was personally sympathetic to Zionism, he recognised the need to assuage Arab fears of unlimited Jewish immigration. A white paper of June 1922, drafted by the British High Commissioner in Palestine, Sir Herbert Samuel, but fully endorsed by Churchill, declared that the "Jewish National Home" did not mean "the imposition of a Jewish nationality upon the inhabitants of Palestine as a whole" but the continued development of the existing Jewish community. ∎

restoration of the gold standard at the pre-war parity of $4.86 to the pound.

As it involved raising the external value of the pound, making British exports more expensive and exporting industries less competitive, the decision was likely to entrench post-war industrial depression and push up unemployment. Churchill therefore approached the decision with great caution. In January 1925 he invited his Treasury officials and the Governor of the Bank of England, Montagu Norman, to reply to an "Exercise" in which he set out possible objections to an early return to gold. It was essential, Churchill explained, that they should be prepared to answer any criticisms.

He himself was not free from doubt. In response to an article by Maynard Keynes in The Nation, he fired off a letter to his Controller of Finance, Otto Niemeyer, which, in the words of Keynes's biographer, Robert Skidelsky, "contained perhaps the most savage indictment of the Treasury and the Bank ever penned by a Chancellor of the Exchequer".[33] The Treasury, Churchill wrote, had never faced the profound significance of what Keynes termed "the paradox of unemployment amidst dearth". The Governor of the Bank

> shows himself perfectly happy in the spectacle of a Britain possessing the finest credit in the world simultaneously with a million and a quarter

unemployed... The seas of history are full of famous wrecks. Still if I could see a way I would far rather follow it than any other. I would rather see Finance less proud and Industry more content.[34]

Torn between rival opinions, Churchill arranged a dinner party at which two protagonists of the return to gold, Niemeyer and Bradbury, argued the case against two of its critics, Keynes and McKenna. Keynes and McKenna argued that it would involve substantial deflation and unemployment, but when Churchill asked McKenna what decision he would make as a politician he replied: "There is no escape. You will have to go back; but it will be hell."[35]

Keynes had lost the argument, but he soon returned to the fray in a pamphlet entitled *The Economic Consequences of Mr Churchill*. He argued that a return to gold at the pre-war parity involved an over-valuation of sterling as a result of which export industries would attempt to reduce their costs by cutting wages. The consequences would be particularly severe for the miners. His judgment was vindicated when the coal owners attempted to force through wage cuts and a national coal strike threatened.

To avert the strike Churchill agreed at the end of June 1925 to subsidise miners' wages for a nine-month period during which proposals for a settlement could be worked out. When the nine months expired without a settlement the general council of the Trade Union Congress went ahead and called the strike, which began on 3 May 1926.

What most worried Churchill was not the dispute in the coal industry but the revolutionary creed of syndicalism – the attempt to use the industrial power of the working class to coerce the government. He was determined, as were Baldwin and the rest of the Cabinet, to break the strike, and if he appeared more militant than the others it was only because he was more rhetorical and demonstrative. Baldwin put him in charge of an emergency government newspaper, the *British Gazette*, to which he contributed unsigned

CHURCHILL AND IRELAND

In the general election of 1918 the Irish rebelled against British rule. Sinn Fein, a nationalist party passionately committed to independence from the United Kingdom, swept to victory everywhere outside Protestant Ulster. They promptly set up a separate Irish Parliament in Dublin, issued a declaration of independence, and initiated a campaign of resistance to British rule. This gradually took on the character of a guerrilla war between the Irish Republican Army (IRA) on the one hand and the Royal Irish Constabulary (RIC), a paramilitary police force, on the other.

Churchill strongly supported Lloyd George's policy of recruiting two paramilitary forces, the "Black and Tans" and the editorials that breathed defiance. When he arranged for troops to convoy supplies from the London docks through the streets, rumour had it that he was itching to put down the strike by military force.

After nine days the strike petered out, but the dispute in the coal industry lingered on, with little attempt by Baldwin to resolve it. In the autumn, while Baldwin was on holiday, Churchill tried to put pressure on the coal owners to settle, but was thwarted by powerful interests in the Conservative Party. Such nuances were lost on the miners, who believed Churchill was once again the villain of the piece, as at Tonypandy. In the coalfields he was remembered into the late 20th century as a

"Auxis", who carried out unofficial reprisals against the IRA, but also murdered some innocent civilians. He was also full of rash ideas for intensifying the conflict, including raising a force of 30,000 Ulstermen to maintain British authority throughout Ireland. His aim, he told the Cabinet, was to achieve a position of strength from which to negotiate constitutional concessions.

In July 1921 Lloyd George called a truce and Churchill was drawn into the subsequent negotiations which led to the Anglo-Irish treaty of 6 December 1921. Determined to drive a hard bargain, he was chiefly responsible for the military clauses of the treaty, which reserved for Britain the use of three naval bases, the "treaty ports". His opposite number in the negotiations was Michael Collins, the leader of the IRA, with whom he established a good working relationship.

As Colonial Secretary, Churchill was now in charge of Anglo-Irish relations during an extremely tense vindictive class warrior.

Although the title of Keynes's pamphlet suggested that Churchill was to blame for the situation, he believed that the Chancellor had been "gravely misled" by his advisers – the Treasury officials and the Governor of the Bank. "Keynes never blamed Winston Churchill personally for the return to gold," writes Robert Skidelsky. "Nor did Churchill take Keynes's attack personally."[36] The political consequences were damaging, with the Conservatives declining in popularity and losing their parliamentary majority in the election of May 1929. Churchill himself in later years came to think of the return to gold as a great mistake, but the person he blamed more than anyone else was the Governor of the Bank of England, Montagu Norman.

period in which there was violence along the border between North and South, and the South itself was descending into civil war. Collins feared that in signing the Treaty he was signing his own death warrant, and so it proved. But shortly before his assassination in August he sent Churchill a message to thank him for all the support he had given to the precarious government of the Irish Free State during its first few troubled months: "Tell Winston that we could never have done anything without him."[37] Churchill felt a sense of paternity towards the Irish Free State and was greatly affronted when De Valera came to power in 1932 and began to abrogate the terms of the Treaty. He was even more incensed in 1938 when Neville Chamberlain returned the 'treaty ports' to Eire, as Ireland was now known. ∎

The rise of Hitler and World War Two

How credible was Churchill as the "Prophet in the Wilderness" of the 1930s?

Churchill has long been famed for his opposition in the 1930s to the appeasement of Nazi Germany. Almost from the moment that Hitler became Chancellor in January 1933 he stood out as the most anti-Nazi of British politicians. He denounced the Nazi police state and its persecution of the Jews, and warned of its aggressive and expansionist aims. He was convinced that Nazi Germany posed a deadly threat to Britain and urged his fellow citizens to do all they could to deter or contain Hitler. In large measure he failed. Neither Baldwin nor Chamberlain was prepared to give him a Cabinet post. Neither was prepared to adopt his policies. In the aftermath of World War Two the explanation appeared obvious, at least to Churchill himself: he had been right and the appeasers wrong; he was prophetic and brilliant, while they were blinkered and mediocre.

But although he was right about the essential character of Nazism, he was not right about everything in the 1930s, nor were the governments of MacDonald, Baldwin and Chamberlain as myopic and foolish as Churchill claimed in his memoirs. It was Robert Rhodes James, in his ground-breaking work, *Churchill: A Study in Failure 1900-1939*, who first pointed out that Churchill bore some of the responsibility for his own isolation. At the root of the problem, he argued, lay the mistrust inspired by Churchill's character:

> We may view with reservation the argument that the fault lay in others, and not in himself. It has become customary to censure those who did not follow his standard; it is therefore appropriate to point out that some responsibility should be attached to the leader whom they refused to follow. [38]

From 1932 to 1935 Churchill and a group of about 50 diehard Tory MPs made a furious and sustained assault on the Government of India Bill, a moderate instalment of constitutional change intended to postpone the question of independence for many years to come. Churchill's India campaign undermined his warnings about Germany. It was not only a huge distraction, absorbing energies which would have been better employed in defence or foreign affairs, but harmful to his reputation. His convictions were genuine but it was evident to anyone in touch with the political realities of India that his judgment was woefully at fault. Nor could the sincerity of his convictions dispel the suspicion that his ultimate aim was to overthrow Baldwin.

Besides, it would be a mistake to imagine that the government was oblivious to the German threat. From February 1934 British defence policy was based on two assumptions: that the ultimate enemy was Germany, and that the government must undertake a rearmament programme, planned for completion by 1939. Like Churchill, the government regarded rearmament in the air as the main priority. But in March 1934 Churchill began to campaign in the House of Commons for "air parity" with Germany. This was an effective way of dramatising the issue, and compelled Baldwin to promise that parity would be maintained, but it turned rearmament into a

---

ON REARMAMENT

"The Government simply cannot make up their minds... So they go on in strange paradox, decided only to be undecided, resolved to be irresolute, adamant for drift... So we go on preparing more months and years – precious perhaps vital to the greatness of Britain – for the locusts to eat."

House of Commons, 12 November 1936

numbers game when the numbers themselves were unreliable. The data on German air strength, secretly supplied to Churchill by sources in the Air Ministry and the RAF, were grossly exaggerated. Nor were numbers as important as capabilities. "Until 1939," writes the historian Richard Overy, "the German air force was no real threat to Britain."[39] The technology of aircraft design was changing rapidly and a large-scale programme of aircraft production in 1934 would have produced a bomber force that was obsolete by 1940.

In the spring of 1936, with the assistance of a secret cross-party organisation known as the "Focus", Churchill began to call for Britain to adopt a foreign policy based on collective security under the League of Nations. By implication this would include the Soviet Union, whose admission to the League he had welcomed in 1934. In his anti-Bolshevik mood of 1919 Churchill would readily have believed the tales of horror trickling out of the Soviet Union, and he may well have believed them in the 1930s. But from 1933 his anti-communism was subordinated to the conviction that Nazi Germany was the greater danger, a military rather than an ideological judgment from which it followed that Britain and the Soviet Union shared a common interest in resisting Hitler. By 1936 he was in regular contact with Ivan Maisky, the Soviet ambassador in London.

Churchill, however, again undermined his

defence campaign by his intervention in the Abdication crisis of December 1936. The new king, Edward VIII, was determined to marry an American divorcee, Wallis Simpson. In the eyes of respectable society the King and his mistress were the leaders of a frivolous and irresponsible set, half-American and wholly undesirable, which threatened to undermine the moral authority of the monarchy. Baldwin told the King that he must either abandon his plan to marry Mrs Simpson or abdicate.

Churchill, who had long been a friend of the King, hoped that he could be persuaded to see the error of his ways; why give up an Empire to make a mistress into a wife? He therefore pleaded in the Commons for the King to be given more time to come to a decision. Egging Churchill on was his

ON GANDHI

'It is alarming and also nauseating to see Mr Gandhi, a seditious Middle Temple lawyer, now posing as a fakir of a type well known in the East, striding half-naked up the steps of the Vice-regal palace, while he is still organising and conducting a defiant campaign of civil disobedience, to parley on equal terms with the representative of the King-Emperor.'

Speech at Epping, 23 February 1931

incorrigibly mischievous friend Lord Beaverbrook, who detested Baldwin and wanted to form a King's Party to overthrow him. It is unlikely that Churchill, who acted throughout with Baldwin's knowledge and consent, was engaged in a plot to seize the premiership, but many, even his friends, concluded that he was.

When Baldwin finally departed in May 1937, Churchill seconded Neville Chamberlain's nomination as leader of the Conservative Party. He respected Chamberlain as the driving force behind rearmament and hoped that he would take a firmer line with Germany. No doubt he was also angling for office, but Chamberlain, who recalled him as a turbulent colleague in the Baldwin Cabinet of 1924 to 1929, was determined to exclude him. Chamberlain also intended to run his own foreign policy, a resolve that drove the Foreign Secretary, Anthony Eden, to resign in February 1938.

Churchill praised Eden, criticised Chamberlain for making concessions to Mussolini, and warned against a policy of appeasing totalitarian powers. But when German troops marched into Austria in March 1938, he expressed in private his sympathy for Chamberlain. Never, he remarked, had a Prime Minister inherited a more ghastly situation, the blame for which rested entirely with Baldwin. The British were faced with an appalling dilemma: "We stand to lose everything by failing to take strong action. Yet if we take strong action, London will be a shambles in half an hour."[40] For their part Eden and his small band of supporters in the House of Commons were careful to keep their distance from Churchill. "Don't be worried my darling," Harold Nicolson assured his wife, Vita Sackville-West, "I am not going to become one of the Winston brigade."[41]

Czechoslovakia, now clearly marked out as the next victim of a German assault, posed an alarming problem for British policy-makers. Both France and the Soviets were pledged to assist Czechoslovakia in the event of a German attack, and if they were to do so Britain would be compelled to join them. The Chiefs of Staff, however, advised that it would be impossible to prevent the Germans from over-running Czechoslovakia. Chamberlain was convinced that in the event of war neither the US nor the Soviet Union could be relied upon to give any effective support. There was, however, a danger that war between Britain and Germany would precipitate attacks by Italy and Japan against the British Empire. Britain did not have the resources with which to combat all three powers at once – as events were to prove.

The moral justification of a war for Czechoslovakia was also in doubt: under the Treaty of Versailles three million German speakers in the Sudetenland, former inhabitants of the Austro-German Empire, had been included without their consent in a state dominated by seven million Czechs and three million Slovaks. Many of the Sudetenlanders were fervent supporters of the local

Nazi movement, which demanded autonomy for the German-speaking population. Had Britain and France the right to deny self-determination to the Sudetenlanders?

In the spring of 1938 both Chamberlain and Churchill hoped that a crisis could be averted by putting pressure on the Czechs to concede autonomy to the Sudetenland. Churchill, in the meantime, urged the government to collaborate with France in gathering together as many European states as possible – the Soviet Union included – for mutual defence under the banner of the League of Nations. Chamberlain, however, had no faith in the plan and continued his quest for appeasement.

By the beginning of September 1938 hopes of an internal solution to the Czech question were fading fast. Determined to avoid war at almost any price, Chamberlain flew three times to Germany in an attempt to find some diplomatic formula that would enable Hitler to obtain by agreement what he was threatening to obtain by force. After the second meeting he came back with terms so humiliating that the Cabinet rejected them. War appeared to be imminent, the paths of Chamberlain and Churchill converging. But the Munich conference of 29 September, convened at the last possible moment by Mussolini, enabled Chamberlain and his French opposite number Daladier to act out a charade of negotiations while agreeing to the immediate transfer of the

Sudetenland to Germany. In the course of the crisis Churchill had warned Chamberlain and Halifax on three different occasions to stand firm.

Chamberlain returned home from Munich to a hero's welcome. Carried away by euphoria, he told the cheering crowd outside Number 10 that it was "the second time in our history that there has come back from Germany to Downing Street peace with honour. I believe it is peace in our time."[42] But Munich had opened up a chasm between Chamberlain and Churchill, who was appalled by the shame of a humiliating surrender and the loss of a strategic bastion. He denounced Chamberlain's policy root and branch. "I will begin," he said,

> by saying what everybody would like to ignore or forget but which must nevertheless be stated, namely that we have suffered a total and unmitigated defeat... This is only the first sip, the first foretaste of a bitter cup which will be proffered to us year by year unless by a supreme recovery of moral health and martial vigour, we arise again and take our stand for freedom as in the olden time. [43]

The House, thought Leo Amery, was "really impressed" by Churchill's speech.[44] But the more effective his attacks, the stronger the backlash that followed. Apart from Duff Cooper, who had caused a sensation by resigning from the government in protest, Churchill was by far the most prominent and outspoken of the small band of Tory MPs who had abstained in the division at the end of the Munich debate. The winter of 1938–9 was the true period of his exile in the wilderness. Ostracised by his own party, he narrowly survived a vote of confidence in his constituency association. But as Churchill himself was aware, his isolation and his prophecies of doom might yet turn out to be the title deeds of his restoration. "By this time next year," he wrote in November 1938, "we shall know whether the Prime Minister's view of Herr Hitler and the German Nazi Party is right or wrong. By this time next year we shall know whether the policy of appeasement has appeased, or whether it has only stimulated a more ferocious appetite."[45]

How did Churchill become prime minister?

When war broke out in September 1939 Churchill had been out of office for ten years. But his warnings against the Nazis had been vindicated and he knew more about waging war than anyone else in politics. Unable to resist the growing cross-party movement for his restoration to office, Chamberlain brought him into his War Cabinet as First Lord of the Admiralty. Against the

Churchill during the election campaign in London, 1935

background of a lacklustre ministerial team of unwarlike old gentlemen, Churchill's confidence and fighting spirit stood out. Cinema audiences cheered when he appeared on the newsreels. But senior figures in both the Conservative and Labour parties still doubted whether he would make a good Prime Minister. As ever, they feared that he "lacked judgment" and would drive the War Cabinet in dangerous directions. Their preferred candidate was the Foreign Secretary Lord Halifax, whose nickname the "Holy Fox" derived from his devotion to hunting and high Anglicanism.

Churchill repeatedly urged the War Cabinet to

mine Norwegian territorial waters in order to block the winter supply route of iron ore from Narvik to Germany. After long delays the waters were mined in April 1940, but the Allied move was overtaken almost at once by a German invasion of Denmark and Norway. The British despatched an ill-prepared expedition to Norway, which failed to oust the Germans and had to be evacuated at the end of April.

The extent of Churchill's responsibility for this humiliating defeat is a matter on which historians differ. The most recent assessment, by the naval historian Christopher Bell, argues that it was Chamberlain and Halifax rather than Churchill who bungled the operation. Whatever the truth, it was Chamberlain who suffered the backlash of anger and humiliation. When the Commons debated the Norway campaign on 7 and 8 May 1940, Churchill spoke loyally in favour of Chamberlain, but the Conservative elder statesman Leo Amery took the lead in a rebellion of backbench Tory MPs against the Prime Minister. He quoted the words Oliver Cromwell had used in dismissing the Long Parliament in 1653: "You have sat too long here for any good you have been doing. Depart, I say, and let us have done with you. In the name of God, go!"[47\]

When the Labour Party challenged Chamberlain by dividing the House, 39 Tory MPs voted against the government and several others abstained, reducing the government's majority from the normal figure of around 200 to 81. Chamberlain tried to regain the confidence of the House by broadening his government, but Labour refused to serve under him and the Tory rebels declared that they would only support an all-party government.

Recognising that he would have to resign, Chamberlain summoned a meeting on 9 May to decide who he should recommend to the King as his successor. Only four people were present: Chamberlain himself, the Conservative Chief Whip, David Margesson, and the two candidates for the premiership, Churchill, and the Foreign Secretary, Lord Halifax. Chamberlain indicated that Halifax would be more likely to win the confidence of the Labour party. Margesson stressed the need for unity but without declaring for either candidate. Here was the opportunity for Churchill to concede the premiership to Halifax, which he might have done but for the advice of two men who had urged him strongly in advance not to: his devoted follower Brendan Bracken, and the owlish Lord Privy Seal Kingsley Wood, formerly a loyal Chamberlainite. By remaining silent Churchill indicated that he wanted the premiership and it was Halifax who made a little speech of renunciation.

At dawn on 10 May the Germans invaded the Low Countries and Chamberlain made a brief but futile bid to remain at his post. That evening

George VI appointed Churchill as Prime Minister. He at once invited the Labour and Liberal parties to join a coalition government under his leadership, and set up a War Cabinet of only five members: himself, the leaders of the Conservative and Labour parties, Chamberlain and Attlee, and their seconds-in-command, Lord Halifax and Arthur Greenwood. "I felt as if I were walking with destiny" Churchill wrote in his war memoirs, "and that all my past life had been but a preparation for this hour and for this trial".[47]

How did he establish himself in power?

In hindsight Churchill looks like an impregnable war leader. It seems unthinkable that his authority can ever have been in doubt, inconceivable that he could have been overthrown. At the time, however, his succession to the premiership was only a staging post in the struggle for power. The reason he appears in retrospect to have been so indispensable is that he fought so hard to ensure he was, and won.

Most Prime Ministers take office as the victor in a general election and leader of the largest party in the House of Commons. Churchill was neither. There were very few Churchillians in the government because there were very few Churchillians at all. During the first few weeks of his premiership, Conservative MPs continued to give a warm reception to Chamberlain when he entered the debating chamber, but cold-shouldered Churchill.

Nor did Churchill have an immediately plausible strategy to offer. When he first addressed the House of Commons as Prime Minister, on 13 May 1940, he said:

> You ask, what is our aim? I can answer in one word: It is victory, victory at all costs, victory in spite of all terror, victory, however long and hard the road may be; for without victory, there is no survival.[48]

These brave words were nothing less than a pledge to reverse the course of history: since 1933 Hitler had achieved success after success. He had remilitarised the Rhineland, marched his troops into Austria, annexed the Sudetenland, occupied the remainder of Czechoslovakia, invaded Poland and partitioned it with the Soviet Union. In April 1940 he had occupied Denmark and Norway. In May he had overrun the Low Countries and swept through France towards Paris. By the third week of May French forces were in full retreat and the Nazis were driving the British Expeditionary Force back towards Dunkirk where it was threatened with encirclement and capture.

Realism suggested that Hitler had won the war and that there was little or nothing the British could do about it. Such was the position on the afternoon of 26 May when the Foreign Secretary, Lord Halifax, proposed in the secrecy of the War Cabinet that Britain and France should invite Italy, which had not yet entered the war, to act as a mediator between Germany and the Allies in a peace settlement. Halifax said that if "we could obtain terms that did not postulate the destruction of our independence, we should be foolish if we did not accept them". Churchill argued passionately that the odds against Hitler offering terms that did not leave Britain at his mercy were a thousand to one, and that Britain was more likely to get better terms later on. Halifax pressed hard, threatening resignation if Churchill would not agree. He confessed in his diary that "it does drive one to despair when he works himself up into a passion of emotion when he ought to make his brain think and reason".[49]

Over three days the War Cabinet debated the issue. Churchill could at least rely on the support of the two Labour leaders, Attlee and Greenwood, and the leader of the Liberals, his old friend "Archie" Sinclair, who was not a member of the War Cabinet but was entitled to attend when invited by the Prime Minister. It was Chamberlain, however, who finally tipped the balance in

Churchill's favour on 28 May. To reinforce his victory Churchill summoned a meeting of 25 ministers outside the War Cabinet and declared: "If this long island story of ours is to end at last, let it end only when each one of us lies choking in his own blood upon the ground."[50] Within a few days the bulk of the BEF had been successfully evacuated from Dunkirk.

For the time being Chamberlain and Halifax remained in the War Cabinet as the guardians of the Conservative party. In October, however, cancer forced Chamberlain to retire. Churchill decided to assume the leadership of the party and with it control of a substantial majority in the House of Commons. As he explained in his war memoirs,

> I would have found it impossible to conduct the war if I had had to procure the agreement in the compulsive days of crisis and during the long years of adverse and baffling struggle not only of the leaders of the two minority parties but of the leader of the Conservative majority. Whoever had been chosen and whatever his self-denying virtues, he would have had the real political power. [51]

Shortly afterwards Churchill was able to dispose of Halifax as well by sending him to Washington as British ambassador to the US.

By a process of trial and error Churchill

delegated authority over the war economy to Ernest Bevin as Minister of Labour and Sir John Anderson as Lord President of the Council along with an assortment of businessmen and party politicians. He was sometimes criticised for neglecting the home front but his authority as Prime Minister stemmed ultimately from his role as a warrior whose mission was to turn defeat into victory.

Could he deliver that victory? Between May 1940 and November 1942 Britain suffered a long series of defeats and disasters punctuated only by victory in the Battle of Britain (July to October 1940) and occasional advances in the western desert. The entry of the Soviet Union into the war in June 1941 raised the spectre of a German victory in the East. And although Pearl Harbor brought the United States into the war in December 1941, the immediate consequences for Churchill were humiliating: on 10 December the *Prince of Wales* and the *Repulse*, the warships Churchill had sent to the Far East to deter Japanese aggression, were sunk by the Japanese off the coast of Malaya. Then February 1942 brought one of the greatest military disasters in British history, the surrender of Singapore with its garrison of more than 100,000 men. Churchill's political fate now depended on victory in the Middle East, but in June 1942 the British garrison at Tobruk fell to Rommel.

Churchill survived because he was a great

democrat with two major power bases, the House of Commons and popular opinion. The House was the ultimate arbiter of the fate of a politician. No matter how low his fortunes might sink, a speech that impressed and commanded the House would raise him up again. Churchill, who had made a study of the art of rhetoric, was careful to devote many hours to the preparation of his speeches. While they usually included a literary flourish or two, the key to a Churchill speech was the detailed if polemical analysis of an issue. The failure of many of his parliamentary speeches in the 1930s was due mainly to the fact that MPs were opposed to his policies.

In wartime, when Churchill embodied the general will of the House and the country, his formidable debating skills came into their own. When there were rumbles of discontent in January 1942, he demanded a vote of confidence and spoke for an hour and a half in the subsequent debate. "One can actually feel the wind of opposition dropping sentence by sentence," wrote Harold Nicolson in his diary, "and by the time he finishes it is clear that there really is no opposition at all – only a certain uneasiness."[52] Aneurin Bevan, a fierce backbench critic of Churchill and the only politician who came close to matching his firepower in debate, gave the point a cruel twist. "The Prime Minister wins debate after debate'" he observed, "and loses battle after battle."[53]

TEN FACTS ABOUT
WINSTON CHURCHILL

1.
In 1913 Churchill began to have flying lessons and took to the air 150 times before giving up at the request of Clementine, who feared that he would kill himself.

2.
Churchill was a film fan who greatly enjoyed the comedies of Charlie Chaplin and the Marx Brothers. His favourite movie was *Lady Hamilton,* a romance featuring Vivien Leigh in the title role and Laurence Olivier as Nelson.

3.
In a speech in honour of the actress Ellen Terry in 1906 Churchill urged the creation of a state-funded National Theatre.

4.
In 1946 Churchill took up the racing and breeding of racehorses. Over the next few years he bought some 38 horses which ran under the racing colours of his father, Lord Randolph.

5.
He had the gift, he says in his war memoirs, of being able to fall instantly into a deep sleep, which enabled

him to work through until 2am or later. He also used to go to bed for at least an hour as soon after lunch as possible. The habit of taking a siesta was one he had learned on a trip to Cuba in 1895.

6.
When he resigned the premiership in 1955, he declined the Queen's offer to make him a duke.

7.
He was an animal lover who created a menagerie of cats, dogs, pigs, tropical fish, butterflies, and black swans at Chartwell. Among the favourite companions of his later years were Nelson the cat, Rufus the poodle and Toby the budgerigar.

8.
Churchill was initiated into the freemasons in 1901.

9.
On 9 April 1963 he was proclaimed an Honorary Citizen of the United States by President John F. Kennedy. On 22 November he watched in tears the television reports of Kennedy's assassination.

10.
One of Churchill's recreations at Chartwell was bricklaying, which he was taught by a professional bricklayer, Benny Barnes. He built garden walls and a cottage in the grounds – with the aid of Barnes and two of the Chartwell staff.

There was never a concerted movement to oust Churchill from the premiership, but a rival candidate did appear in January 1942 when Sir Stafford Cripps, a wealthy socialist lawyer whom Churchill had appointed as ambassador to Moscow in 1940, returned home with the air of a saviour. The Red Army and the Soviet Union were hugely popular at the time and Cripps basked in the glow of the Anglo-Soviet alliance, for which he was mistakenly given much of the credit. Having been expelled from the Labour Party in 1939 for advocating a Popular Front, he was a non-party figure who attracted followers on the Right as well as the Left. His calls for a more rigorously planned,

THE ICONOGRAPHY OF CHURCHILL

Churchill's words were reinforced by the pugnacious, flamboyant image of a great showman. Bursting with animal spirits, striding through the streets of blitzed cities twirling a hat aloft on a stick, sporting a ten-gallon hat in the North African desert, Churchill was a star of the newsreels. His most famous prop was a large Havana cigar, which he would light and flourish with much ceremony, but seldom smoke, his most famous gesture, the V-sign with the palm of the hand turned outwards.

His wardrobe was eccentric and varied. In addition to his normal Westminster attire of pinstriped suit, waistcoat and bow tie, he appeared at various times in the uniforms of Air Commodore, member of the Royal Yacht Squadron, and Colonel of Hussars. Early on in the war he gave up wearing a dinner jacket in austere and efficient war effort attracted so much applause that Churchill was compelled to include him in the War Cabinet in February 1942. Cripps, however, was now muzzled, the moment passed, and within a month or two he ceased to be talked off as a successor to Churchill.

The unease in Whitehall and Westminster persisted, however. Following the fall of Tobruk a motion of censure was put down on 1 July by a respected backbencher, Sir John Wardlaw-Milne. It was seconded by Admiral Sir Roger Keyes, the hero of a famous exploit in World War One. Between the two of them they bungled the case. Wardlaw-Milne argued that Churchill was

favour of a zip-up "siren" suit, an eccentric version of a working man's overalls.

The most memorable portraits of Churchill in the Second World War were the work of photographers such as Cecil Beaton (1940), showing him at work in the Cabinet Room, and Karsh of Ottawa (1941), who claimed to have captured Churchill's bulldog expression by snatching the cigar from his mouth. The Ministry of Information featured him in a number of famous posters, but it was the cartoonists who made the deepest impression,

pre-eminent among them the New Zealander David Low, whose mockery of Churchill between the wars was supplanted, in a famous cartoon entitled "All Behind You, Winston", by a heroic image of him marching with sleeves rolled up at the head of a mighty column of British people. No less famous in his day was Sidney Strube, a cartoonist for the *Daily Express*. It was he who first drew the head of Churchill on the body of a bulldog (8 June 1940) thus creating a classic wartime image reproduced in numerous Toby jugs. ∎

interfering too much in military operations; Keyes argued that he should interfere more boldly. Much relieved, Churchill mounted a powerful defence and won a vote of confidence by 476 votes to 25.

Churchill was still in danger, or thought he was. If Egypt had been lost, Cripps would have resigned and put himself at the head of the opposition in the House. In the event, the crisis never came to a head: Montgomery inflicted a decisive defeat on Rommel at El Alamein, and Churchill ordered the church bells – silent since 1940 – to be rung in celebration. For the rest of the war his premiership was secure.

Beyond the House, Churchill's ultimate power base was his phenomenal popularity. Between the evacuation from Dunkirk at the end of May, and the start of the Blitz in September 1940, this soared. How and why is still a little mysterious. Can it have been due to the five broadcasts he gave, one of them consisting of only seven sentences, during these crucial weeks? The magnificent phrases were headlined in the press and repeated in news bulletins on the radio. But there was perhaps a deeper factor at work: the interaction between his personal qualities and the public's need for an aggressive war leader. Churchill could not have turned himself into the hero of the hour but for the irrational faith of the majority of the British in the inevitability of victory. He recognised this in his address to both Houses on his 80th birthday, 30 November 1954: "It was a nation and race dwelling all round the globe that had the lion heart. I had the luck to be called upon to give the roar."[54]

Churchill's personal popularity was surprisingly enduring. His approval rating in July 1940 stood at 88 per cent. The lowest of his monthly ratings was 78 per cent, after the fall of Tobruk, the highest point 93 per cent after Montgomery's victory at El Alamein. In April 1945, three months before he and his party were roundly rejected at the polls, it stood at 91 per cent. It is worth remembering admittedly, that the pollsters were not asking people whether they loved or admired Churchill, but only whether they approved of him as Prime Minister.

Between May 1940 and May 1945 Churchill broadcast some 24 times (excluding broadcasts in the USA). As the historian Richard Toye argues, the effects have sometimes been exaggerated. His broadcasts were not always well received and there was a section of the population immune to his eloquence. Still, the wonder is that such an aristocratic figure, so distant both socially and imaginatively from the manual workers of the industrial areas, or the black-coated workers of suburbia, could appeal so effectively to a mass audience. Part of the explanation lies in the fact that his broadcasts were not as infused as we now imagine with romantic rhetoric. They were listened to because they provided information and commentary on the current state of the war and its likely future course.

How good a military strategist was he?

Churchill had been a soldier before he was a politician. He had written several books about military campaigns. At different times he had been the ministerial head of all three armed services. As Prime Minister he appeared in the uniform of all three armed forces. His joy in the conduct of war and excitement in the presence of danger were celebrated. He believed that he understood strategic problems as well or better than his commanders. While he remained in vital respects a civilian, he was the nearest thing to a military ruler that Britain had experienced since Oliver Cromwell. But was he a second Marlborough, a great strategist?

On becoming Prime Minister he took the additional title of Minister of Defence. Although the powers attached to the title were never defined, and there was no Department of Defence, the effect was that he ran the military side of the war with the Chiefs of Staff Committee, where the heads of the three armed forces met every day to co-ordinate strategy and issue instructions. Churchill was punctilious in preserving the machinery of Cabinet government and insisted that military decisions were ratified by the War Cabinet. In practice his colleagues were happy to

leave strategy and operations to him and military decisions were taken by Churchill and the three service chiefs.

The relationship between the three service chiefs and their master, a visionary amateur strategist bombarding them with demands for action, ranged between tense and explosive. Mediating between them was a machiavellian conciliator, General Sir Hastings Ismay (known as "Pug"), who was Churchill's personal representative on the Chiefs of Staff Committee. The liaison was intimate, and Ismay was able to calm tempers on both sides. For his part, Churchill never forgot the lesson of Fisher's resignation in 1915: he never overruled the Chiefs of Staff on a strictly military issue. Yet to the public, who knew nothing of the role of the Chiefs of Staff, he appeared to be a virtual dictator in his field. As the historian A.J.P. Taylor wrote, he "announced losses and victories in the House of Commons, appointed and dismissed generals, admirals and field marshals. The orders to them were issued in his name or with a 'we' that was more regal than collective."[55]

With his buccaneering spirit, colossal energy, and fertile imagination, Churchill drove his professional advisers hard, and sometimes to distraction. His favourite was the First Sea Lord, Admiral Pound, whose dogged loyalty was, however, tempered by devious methods of resistance. It was to Churchill's credit that the chiefs he appointed were strong characters: Sir John Dill as head of the Army in May 1940, Sir Charles Portal as head of the RAF in succession to Newall in October 1940, and Sir Andrew Cunningham in succession to Pound in September 1943. Dill clashed with Churchill once too often and was removed in December 1941, but in his place Churchill appointed Sir Alan Brooke, of whom he remarked: "When I thump the table and push my face towards him, what does he do? Thumps the table harder and glares back at me."[56] Over and above his daily face-to-face dealings with the service chiefs, Churchill also communicated directly with senior commanders in the field. Impatient for victory, he repeatedly prodded his commanders in the Middle East to undertake offensives, sacking Wavell in 1941 and Auchinleck in 1942 when they failed to deliver.

Within a fortnight of taking over as Prime Minister Churchill acquired "a source of undreamed-of power; knowledge to use against the unsuspecting enemy, but also a trump card in his negotiations with his Chiefs of Staff and allies".[57] On 22 May the code breakers at Bletchley Park broke the main operational key of the Luftwaffe's Enigma enciphering machine. This marked the beginning of Ultra, the daily flow of transcripts of radio messages sent by the German armed forces. Though Ultra was continuously monitored by the Joint Intelligence Committee, whose reports were made available to senior commanders as well as to the Chiefs of Staff, Churchill insisted that he should have direct and independent access to the raw materials. In September 1940 the head of the Secret Intelligence Service, Sir Stewart Menzies, was instructed to send all the original transcripts in a daily box to the Prime Minister. As the volume of transcripts grew, Churchill authorised Menzies to send him a selection only, but he continued to receive a box of what he called his "golden eggs" almost every day of the war.

The many rows between Churchill on the one hand, and the Chiefs of Staff and senior commanders on the other, tend to distract attention from the common ground between them. After the fall of France, and so long as Britain and the Empire stood alone, there was no possibility of a major ground offensive against Germany. Commando raids, which Churchill encouraged, were for moral rather than military effect. When Italy declared war on Britain on 10 July 1940 a new theatre of operations opened up in the Middle East. The British now had a surrogate enemy to fight and a British base in Egypt from which to operate. Opportunism, as much as imperialism, led Churchill and the service chiefs to adopt a "Mediterranean strategy" with the defeat of the Italians in North Africa as the immediate aim. In August 1940 and at great risk to home defence, Churchill sent 154 tanks to Egypt to reinforce

Wavell, the British commander-in-chief.

When Greece was invaded by Germany in March 1941, Churchill accepted the advice of Eden and Wavell and sent in British and Commonwealth troops, but in April Greece was overrun. In May Crete in turn was invaded and captured and British forces again evacuated. Meanwhile, German panzer divisions under the command of Rommel had arrived in North Africa. When a British counter-offensive failed in June 1941 Churchill ran out of patience with Wavell and replaced him as C-in-C Middle East with General Claud Auchinleck. During the autumn of 1941 Churchill bombarded the Chiefs of Staff with proposals, which they stoutly resisted, for landings on the coasts of Norway, Sicily, Italy, and French North Africa. Conversely he paid little attention to the Far East, discounting the idea that Japan would dare to attack the United States or the British Empire. Even if they did attack, he believed, the defences of Singapore would be strong enough to withstand assault for at least six months.

Churchill's impulsive and intuitive mind, fluttering like a butterfly from one attractive prospect to another, caused widespread alarm among senior officers in both the Navy and the Army. The Director of Naval Operations, Captain Ralph Edwards, wrote in the autumn of 1941: "If only the honourable gentleman were to confine himself to statesmanship and politics and leave naval strategy to those properly concerned, the chances of winning the war would be greatly enhanced. He is without doubt one of history's worst strategists."[58] Brooke, the head of the Army, frequently expressed his frustration with Churchill in the secrecy of his diaries. "He cannot grasp the relationship of various theatres of war to each other," he wrote in May 1943. "He always gets carried away by the one he is examining and in prosecuting it is prepared to sacrifice most of the others."[59] Brooke was not alone in his view. Ismay's assistant, Sir Ian Jacob, a great admirer of Churchill, wrote:

> One is bound to question whether Churchill could be classed as a strategist at all. He was certainly not the calm, self-contained, calculating personality that is usually brought to mind by the term, nor did he weigh up carefully the resources available to us, the possible courses open to the enemy, and then, husbanding and concentrating his forces, strike at the selected spot. His mind would never be content with such theoretical ideas. He wanted constant action on as wide a scale as possible; the enemy must be made continually to 'bleed and burn', a phrase he often used.[60]

This pattern of challenge and response, with Churchill demanding sideshows and the service chiefs trying to prevent them, persisted throughout the war. Max Hastings, however, warns us against the uncritical acceptance of Alanbrooke's point of view

> For most of the Second World War Churchill was obliged to struggle against his military advisers' fear of battlefield failure, which in 1942 had become almost obsessive. Alan Brooke was a superbly gifted officer, who forged a remarkable partnership with Churchill. But if Allied operations had advanced at a pace dictated by the War Office, or indeed by Brooke himself, the conflict's ending would have come much later than it did. The British had grown so accustomed to poverty of resources, shortcomings of battlefield performance, that it had become second nature for them to fear the worst. Churchill himself, by contrast, shared with the Americans a desire to hasten forward Britain's creaky military machine. [61]

Churchill's most important contribution to British strategy was the area bombing of German cities, a policy inspired by his scientific adviser, the German-born Professor Lindemann, favoured by the Air Ministry, and executed by "Bomber" Harris, the C-in-C of Bomber Command from February 1942. At the time it was controversial because it diverted aircraft from the antisubmarine war in the Atlantic. Since the war it has been denounced on the grounds that the deliberate targeting of civilians constituted a war crime. Churchill says little about it in his memoirs: evidently it was not a campaign with which he wished to be too closely associated.

Did Churchill pay too high a price for Britain's alliance with the US?

It used to be thought that one of Churchill's greatest achievements was the part he played in the creation of the Anglo-American alliance of 1941-5, "the partnership that saved the West". There is still much to be said for this view. Britain would never have emerged on the winning side of World War Two without the economic aid of the US or the engagement of its armed forces in the liberation of western Europe.

Many of those round Churchill, however, believed he put too much faith in his great "friend", President Roosevelt. Among the sceptics was the Foreign Secretary, Anthony Eden. Could not Churchill see that although the Americans were allies in the short run, they were rivals whose long-term objective was to supersede Britain as a world power? The doubts about Roosevelt were later echoed by post-war historians like John Grigg.

Though he was Britain's loyal ally in the war against Hitler, he was no friend at all to Britain's interests in the world. Indeed, it is strictly true to say that even Hitler was less hostile to the British Empire than he was. It was, therefore, the ultimate in self-deception on Churchill's part to imagine that he could call in the New World to make the British Empire viable and respectable.[62]

Churchill did indeed deceive himself, as Grigg argues. The fantasy he cherished was of pre-war and even perhaps Edwardian origin. He believed that one day the British Empire and the US would be reunited through a common citizenship, a common currency, and constitutional arrangements that wisely he never attempted to define. If the "English-speaking peoples" ever chose to act as one, the Pax Britannica of the 19th century would be replaced by the Pax Anglo-American of the 20th, thus ensuring a peaceful, prosperous and progressive world. But while this was Churchill's long-held romantic ideal, his short-term objective, plainly enough, was to reconcile the US to the continued existence of the British Empire and even to guarantee its future.

When Churchill took over as Prime Minister in May 1940 he was almost immediately plunged by the fall of France into a new phase of Anglo-American relations and during this phase Churchill's mood, for the most part, was one of sombre realism. As David Reynolds writes:

> For domestic consumption he stressed that US
> help was imminent, yet in secret he remained
> disappointed at the lack of assistance, and even
> suspicious that America was waiting to pick up
> the pieces. The doubts and fears led him to
> advocate a tough bargaining approach to the
> USA, tailoring British concessions to tangible
> evidence of American help.[63]

In the early months of Churchill's premiership,
before Roosevelt's re-election in November,
relations between Britain and the United States
were strained on both sides. In Washington it was
suspected that Britain would be defeated, as the
US ambassador in London, Joseph Kennedy, kept
predicting. In which case why send supplies that
the United States might need for its own defence?
Besides, isolationism was still strong in America
and Roosevelt was wary of taking any action that
could be interpreted as entangling his country in a
European war.

For his part, Churchill was in two minds about
Roosevelt. Sometimes he imagined, quite
mistakenly, that Roosevelt was about to bring the
US into the war in alliance with Britain. At other
times he was fearful that the Americans were just
waiting by to pick up the debris of the British
Empire. In his more realistic moods Churchill

understood that Roosevelt would only aid Britain if Britain proved that it was determined to fight on and win. This, of course, was Churchill's policy in any case – and defiant actions, such as the bombing of the French fleet at Oran to prevent it falling into enemy hands, matched his defiant words.

Churchill knew that it was in the strategic interests of the US to sustain British resistance but his bargaining power was weak. Under the destroyers-for-bases agreement of September 1940 Roosevelt promised Britain 50 ancient destroyers in return for a 99-year lease on British bases in the West Indies, Newfoundland and Bermuda – a case of a great imperialist power parting with its assets for a song. Nor did Lend-Lease, hugely welcome thought it was, relieve Churchill's anxieties about America. In the autumn of 1941 his great fear was that its entry into the war would come too late for Britain. In the end the Japanese solved the problem by attacking Pearl Harbor.

The formal entry of the US into the war transformed the relationship with Washington almost overnight into an exceptionally close alliance in which military operations were jointly planned and executed. "In addition to the Combined Chiefs of Staff," writes Warren Kimball, "the concept of a world-wide system of theater commands – a single officer in each theatre commanding the military forces of both the United

States and Great Britain, is unique in modern military annals."[64]

This extraordinary alliance was never free from tensions but it was animated from the top by the President and the Prime Minister, who established a relationship of exceptional intimacy. Were they friends? Yes in the sense that they enjoyed one another's company and had much in common. As Jon Meacham writes, they "loved tobacco, strong drink, history, the sea, battleships, hymns, pageantry, patriotic poetry, high office, and hearing themselves talk".[65] They certainly worked closely together – they exchanged more than 1,700 messages, held 11 bilateral meetings and spent 113 days together over the course of the war. Churchill remarked later: "No lover ever studied the whims of his mistress as I did those of President Roosevelt." [66]

Between 1941 and 1943 Britain had more troops engaged in battle in Europe than the Americans, enabling Churchill to take the lead in Anglo-American operations. Roosevelt and his advisers had decided after Pearl Harbor that the United States should pursue a Europe-first strategy, which of course was music to Churchill's ears. The American Joint Chiefs wanted to give priority to plans for a cross-Channel invasion in 1943. It was Churchill through his influence over Roosevelt who drew them into North Africa and the Mediterranean. There was a high level of co-operation in other fields as well. After much hard bargaining secret intelligence was pooled and British and American code-breakers worked side by side.

In August 1941 Churchill had authorised a top-secret programme of research, code-named "Tube Alloys", into the production of a British atom bomb. Similar research was already in progress in the US and Churchill pressed hard for the pooling and sharing of resources in the 'Manhattan Project'. He was delighted when Roosevelt, overriding much resistance on the American side, signed an agreemen to this effect at Quebec in August 1943.

To Churchill it seemed as if the seeds of his ideal Anglo-American world order were at last springing up all around him. In May 1943, at a British Embassy lunch in Washington, he told American officials he wanted to see a post-war world in which citizens of the British Commonwealth and the US enjoyed common citizenship and the right to live anywhere in each other's territories. Desmond Morton, for many years a close confidante of Churchill, believed he was driven by a psychological compulsion, "all his life torn between his pride in his great Marlborough ancestor... and his love for his Yankee mother. His overpowering ambition was to amalgamate the two; to be made whole through the emergence of one vast English-speaking people." [67]

Churchill unveiled his vision of Anglo-American

union in a speech at Harvard in September 1943, though, ironically, this came at a time when relations between the two countries were increasingly strained. After the Allied invasion of Sicily serious differences arose over the relative importance of an Italian campaign and other initiatives in the Mediterranean on the one hand, and a cross-Channel invasion on the other. The tensions were paralleled by a divergence of view between Churchill and Roosevelt over how to handle Stalin, tensions which first became apparent at the Teheran conference at the end of 1943.

These differences have to be put in perspective. The Normandy landings of June 1944, one of the greatest military operations in history, were the triumphant outcome of Anglo-American planning and co-operation. The alliance, nevertheless, was in decline. In 1943 the United States overtook Britain in the total volume of its munitions output. In 1944 it overtook Britain in terms of the number of Army divisions in fighting contact with the enemy. The balance of power was shifting in America's favour at the very time that contentious post-war issues were emerging. As Churchill discovered at the Teheran conference in December 1943, and again at Yalta in February 1945, Roosevelt's plans for the post-war world were based on an understanding between the US and the Soviet Union. "When I was at Teheran," he told his old friend Violet Bonham-Carter,

I realised for the first time what a very small country this is. On the one hand the big Russian bear with its paw outstretched – on the other the great American Elephant – & between them the poor little British donkey – who is the only one who knows the right way home.[68]

In the disputes that arose between London and Washington over the shape of the post-war world Churchill was far from submissive and his relationship with the President cooled, which may have been the reason why he failed attend Roosevelt's funeral in April 1945.

Churchill did place too much faith in American good will towards Britain. His hopes of converting it into the foundation of a new world order proved illusory. The war aims of the United States included the liquidation of the British Empire and the expansion of American commerce at the expense of British competitors. Nothing, however, should detract from the outstanding role Churchill played in the creation, between 1940 and 1943, of an alliance that ensured the survival of Britain and the liberation of western Europe.

EUROPE IN 1942

Norway

Denmark

Ireland

Great Britain

Netherlands

Germany

Belgium

26

Switzerland

France

Portugal

Italy

Spain

Morocco

Algeria

Tunisia

* The General Government was the area of central and sou
was what remained of Poland after territory in the west had
Germans attacked Russia in June 1941 they overran the Sov
avoided the word 'Poland' as much as possible since they w

...d administered directly by the Nazis from October 1939. It
...d by Germany and territory in the east by Russia. When the
...expanded the General Government to include it. The Nazis
...ned to wipe it out as a nation, hence the anonymous term.

Did Churchill make too many concessions to Stalin?

Churchill's dealings with the Soviet Union touched on a dilemma at the heart of his war leadership. He had been a passionate opponent of Communism. When, however, Hitler invaded Russia on 22 June 1941, he embraced the Soviet Union as an ally for compelling military reasons. Between 1941 and 1943 Churchill's attitudes to Stalin were shaped by the fear that the Nazis would succeed in conquering the Soviet Union, or that Stalin in desperation would be driven to make peace with Hitler. If either of these things happened the Nazis would be free once more to turn the might of their forces against Britain. Hence the policy he announced in a broadcast on the day of the invasion: "Any man or state who fights on against Nazidom will have our aid."[69]

In September 1941 an Anglo-American mission to Moscow pledged the British and American governments to send thousands of aircraft, tanks, and other supplies to Russia. Churchill also gave instructions that secret intelligence about German activities on the Eastern Front be passed on to Stalin. Stalin, fearing the Allies would leave the Soviet Union to bear the brunt of the war, was far from satisfied and demanded, sometimes rudely and aggressively, that the British and the Americans should launch a second front in

Europe. To reassure him, Churchill flew to Moscow in August 1942.

Once the Soviet Union had beaten off the Nazi attack and began to advance into eastern Europe Churchill had a new fear – that the Red Army would carry communism into the heart of Europe. He knew that Stalin was a cruel and brutal tyrant and the author of many atrocities. But he never wavered from the overriding goal of defeating Nazi Germany and he showed no interest whatever in the idea of a compromise peace in order to forestall the Soviet advance. He therefore continued to treat Stalin as an ally, though he remarked in February 1944: "If my shirt were taken off now it would be seen that my belly is sore from crawling to that man. I do it for the good of the country and for no other reason."[70]

At the heart of his dilemma lay the problem of Poland, the nation for which, ostensibly, the British had gone to war in 1939. The exiled Polish government in London was deeply anti-Soviet and determined to recover the territories occupied by the Soviet Union. The British, however, could not afford to alienate a major ally for the sake of a lesser one. At the Teheran Conference in late 1943 Churchill had told Stalin that the Poles would be made to accept a loss of territory in the east in return for which they would receive compensation in the form of German territory in the west.

In January 1944, as the Red Army fought its

way into Poland, Stalin set up the Lublin Committee, a body of Soviet puppets, to administer the "liberated" territories. It was clear that he would be in a position to impose whatever settlement he wished on Poland. Churchill therefore urged the Polish government in exile to accept the revised frontiers and enter into discussions with the Lublin Committee, but they had other ideas. They were busy planning an uprising by the Polish underground army to seize control of Warsaw in advance of the entry of Soviet troops.

By the end of July Soviet troops were on the outskirts of Warsaw. The rising began on 1 August. Over the next three months the Polish army fought a desperate battle in which they were brutally and remorselessly destroyed by the Nazis. Soviet troops failed to intervene. Stalin condemned the Polish fighters as criminal adventurers and refused to drop arms supplies by air. He also refused American aircraft permission to make use of airfields in the Soviet Union for the same purpose. Churchill and the War Cabinet were alarmed by Stalin's attitude and distressed by the fate of the rising, but powerless to intervene. "Terrible and humbling submissions must at times be made to the general aim," Churchill wrote in his war memoirs.[71]

Churchill reverted to the idea of a settlement with Stalin. On his second visit to Moscow in October 1944 he wrote out on a single sheet of paper a proposal for the division of the Balkan

The "Big Three" at the Yalta Conference: Winston Churchill, Franklin D. Roosevelt, and Joseph Stalin, 4-11 February 1945

countries into spheres of influence expressed in percentages. Romania, for example, was to be 90 per cent in the Russian sphere and 10 per cent in the British; Greece 90 per cent British and 10 per cent Russian. Stalin read the paper, put a large tick on it, and handed it back. For Churchill the most important feature of the agreement was the promise that Greece would be saved from communism. "I have had very nice talks with the Old Bear," Churchill wrote to his wife. "I like him the more I see of him. Now they respect us here & I am sure they wish to work with us."[72]

In December 1944, Churchill's optimism was confirmed by events in Greece. When German forces withdrew from the country in October 1944 Churchill sent in a British occupying force under

General Ronald Scobie with orders to support the provisional government of Papandreou. Greece, however, was on the brink of a civil war between monarchist forces loyal to the exiled King George II, and the communist controlled EAM (National Liberation Front) and its guerrilla wing ELAS (People's National Army of Liberation). On 3 December fighting broke out between ELAS and the police in Athens and ELAS seized control of the city.

In the knowledge that he had Stalin's permission to act, Churchill gave full rein to his anti-communist convictions and ordered General Scobie to suppress EAM-ELAS. "We have to hold and dominate Athens," Churchill wrote. "It would

WAS CHURCHILL A RACIST?

The answer is "yes" – up to a point. In his defence it can be said that he viewed history as a record of the rise and fall of civilisations and recognised that one day the British Empire, too, would fall. He had no use for biological theories of race and employed the word as a cultural term, a synonym for "people". Proud though he was of his Englishness, he knew that the English were, as Defoe had called them, "a mongrel race". Half American himself, he believed that his mother, Lady Randolph, was partly of Native American descent. He never preached racial hatred and was almost completely immune to anti-Semitism at a time when it was rife. On the contrary, he was a conspicuous ally of Jews and Zionists. All these things can be said in his defence but he be a great thing for you to succeed in this without bloodshed if possible, but also with bloodshed if necessary."[73] To his great embarrassment the telegram leaked and he was strongly criticised both at home and in the US. There was, however, not a word of protest from Stalin: deeply impressed and grateful, Churchill drew the conclusion that he could trust the Russian dictator.

When the "Big Three" assembled at the Yalta conference (4 to 11 February 1945) the future of Poland was the most awkward problem on the agenda. Stalin promised to allow free elections in Poland and Churchill, encouraged by his behaviour over Greece, tried his best to believe him. "Poor Neville believed he could trust Hitler,"

---

was, nonetheless, a racist of a kind and his racism did inform his politics.

Churchill's racial attitudes were framed by late Victorian imperialism and embedded into his outlook by personal experience. While still in his twenties he fought the Pathans of north-west India, and the Dervishes of the Sudan, where he charged with the 21st Lancers at the Battle of Omdurman. His was a social Darwinian view of the world in which the more progressive races, of whom

the British were first and foremost, were destined to conquer Asian and African peoples and confer on them the blessings of disinterested paternal rule. After a tour of east Africa as Colonial Under-Secretary he wrote

No one can travel even for a little while among the Kikuyu tribes without acquiring a liking for these light-hearted, tractable, if brutish children, or without feeling that they are capable of being instructed and

Churchill told his ministers. "He was wrong. But I don't think I'm wrong about Stalin."[74] When the Commons debated the Yalta agreement on 28 February, Churchill declared: "I know of no Government which stands to its obligation, even to its own despite, more solidly than the Russian Soviet Government."[75] As in the debate over Greece, Churchill's speech demonstrated that he still possessed the power to dominate the Commons, but he was attacked by some Conservative MPs for sacrificing Polish territory and the arguments on which he relied awoke memories of the case for Munich as argued by Chamberlain and his supporters. In the division on

raised from their present degradation... It will be an ill day for these native races when their fortunes are removed from the impartial and august administration of the Crown and abandoned to the fierce self-interest of a small white population.[77]

The historian Ronald Hyam wrote of the young Churchill: 'He had a generous and sensitive, if highly paternalistic sympathy for subject peoples, and a determination to see that justice was done to humble individuals

throughout the empire.'[78]

In the aftermath of World War One, as Churchill's world-view became more pessimistic, his attitude towards African and Asian peoples shifted from enlightened to embittered paternalism. The most obvious explanation lies in his realisation that the Empire was in decline, undermined first of all by nationalism in Ireland and India, but also by growing pressure at home for concessions to nationalism. Perhaps, too, the frustration of his own ambitions played a part. By the 1940s his private

1 March, 25 Conservative MPs voted against the government. Churchill's private secretary detected seeds of doubt in his master's mind: "He is trying to persuade himself that all is well, but in his heart I think he is worried about Poland and not convinced of the strength of our moral position." [76]

In Poland, Stalin's agents were busy weeding out and liquidating potential opponents. Churchill was greatly alarmed and in a last-ditch attempt to contain Soviet expansionism implored Roosevelt and Eisenhower, the Supreme Allied Commander, to change their military plans to prevent the Russians from getting to Berlin before the British and the Americans. They refused, and Harry

comments were sour and pejorative. As the historian Christopher Thorne has noted, Churchill could launch into a most terrible attack on the "'baboos', saying that they were 'gross, dirty and corrupt'...or talk of 'not letting the Hottentots by popular vote throw the white people into the sea'".[79] "The P.M." noted Jock Colville, Churchill's private secretary, in 1945, "said the Hindus were a foul race 'protected by their mere pullulation from the doom that is their due' and he wished Bert Harris could send some of his surplus bombers to destroy them."[80]

For such a remark, even if it was only said in private, no defence is possible, and there were numerous asides of a similar character. The best plea in mitigation of Churchill's racial attitudes is that they were commonplace in the age of imperialism in which he had grown up. And if there was a streak of brutality in his world-view it was a streak that also fuelled his obstinate refusal to acquiesce in the decline of Britain as a great power and drove his opposition to appeasement. ∎

Truman, who took over as president following Roosevelt's death on 12 April, insisted on leaving the decision to Eisenhower. The Red Army, as originally planned, captured Berlin and Prague.

So great was Churchill's fear of Soviet expansionism that he even instructed the Chiefs of Staff to draw up contingency plans for an Anglo-American war against the Soviet Union, "Operation Unthinkable". It was indeed unthinkable, as Churchill himself must have realised – if the military aspects were discouraging, the political difficulties were insurmountable. It would have been impossible to rally support for confrontation with an ally which had accumulated such vast reserves of gratitude and admiration.

Churchill's pessimism was alleviated to some degree when Truman took him aside at Potsdam and gave him the news of the successful testing of the atom bomb in New Mexico. For the time being, at least, the Americans had the bomb and the Russians did not. "If the Russians had got it, it would have been the end of civilisation," Churchill told his doctor, Lord Moran.[81] "It has just come in time to save the world." Nevertheless Churchill could see clearly enough that whereas Britain had been the leading world power up to 1939, it had now been overtaken by two superpowers, one that was threatening to dominate Europe, and one that was threatening to retreat into isolationism.

Conservative political tradition. He could have devolved the task to others in order to maintain his concentration on the war. In the event he did none of these things but made unconvincing promises for the future while leaving the impression that he and his party were anti-Beveridge. He assumed, of course, as most people did, that he was bound to win the first post-war general election.

In the general election of 1945 Churchill had no message for the electorate, party political or otherwise. In a vain attempt to fill the vacuum he came up with a stunt. In the opening broadcast of the campaign, on 4 June, he warned that the introduction of socialism into Britain would require "some form of Gestapo, no doubt very humanely directed in the first instance". The allegation was regarded by all but the most loyal of Churchill's followers as outrageous, and retains its notoriety down to the present day – although there is no evidence to suggest that it cost him many votes, still less the election.

In the general election of November 1935 the Conservatives had won with 432 seats and 53.7 per cent of the vote. In the general election of July 1945 Labour won with 393 seats and 47.8 per cent of the total vote. The result plunged Churchill into depression but circumstances were not as grim as they looked at first. The parliamentary majority produced by the first-past-the-post electoral system gave an exaggerated impression of Labour's ascendancy. A majority of voters had in fact voted against Labour, and there was no reason to think that the Conservatives were perpetually doomed. Churchill soon recovered his spirits, reinvented himself as a global statesman, doggedly retained the leadership of the Conservative Party, and confidently awaited what he saw as the inevitable reaction of the British against socialism.

What was Churchill's post-war vision?

Towards the end of 1945 Churchill received an invitation to give one in a series of annual lectures at Westminster College in Fulton, Missouri. There, on 5 March 1946, in the presence of President Truman, he gave the first public warning by a leading British or American statesman of the dangers of Soviet expansionism – in effect, the first public declaration of the Cold War. "From Stettin in the Baltic to Trieste in the Adriatic," he declared, "an iron curtain has descended across the Continent."[82]

By comparison with the warnings he had once given about Nazi Germany his remarks about Russia were, however, comparatively restrained. "I do not believe that Soviet Russia desires war," he said. "What they desire is the fruits of war and the indefinite expansion of their power and doctrines." The only way to prevent this was for the western democracies to stand together, maintain their military strength, and to seek "a good understanding on all points with Russia under the authority of the United Nations Organisation..."[83] This, he argued, was not a prescription for war but for peace. Although the speech is often referred to as the Iron Curtain speech, Churchill gave it the title "The Sinews of Peace".

Churchill attempted to sugar the pill with the argument that his plan would strengthen the authority of the United Nations, but for many commentators the speech raised the spectre of a renewed struggle for world power leading ultimately to World War Three. In Britain the pro-Labour press condemned the speech and 105 Labour MPs signed a motion deploring it. It is difficult now to appreciate the shock it caused – the Soviet Union was still generally thought of in Britain and the US as a wartime ally and a partner in the newly created United Nations.

But inside the British and American governments there were already strong currents of anti-Soviet opinion. Neither Attlee or his Foreign Secretary, Ernest Bevin, received advance copies of the Fulton speech but they had a good idea of the line he was proposing to take and made no attempt to stop him. Truman claimed that he had not read it in advance, but in fact he and Secretary of State James F Byrnes had both read a draft and raised no objections. It served the purposes of both the British and the American governments for Churchill to take the lead by saying in public what high officials were thinking in private. He would take the flak while they stood back and claimed that he was speaking only for himself.

This also suited Churchill. It gave him the opportunity once more of appearing on the world stage in role of prophet as he had in the 1930s. Although in the short run he was strongly attacked, in the longer run he was vindicated by events. By 1949 his views had become widely accepted in the western democracies.

In the Fulton speech, Churchill also floated once more his long-cherished vision of Anglo-American unity, a "fraternal association of the

JOURNALIST AND AUTHOR

If, as Samuel Johnson declared, "abundance is the hallmark of genius", then nowhere was Churchill's genius more apparent than in his literary output. By 1900 he was one of the most celebrated war correspondents of his day. By 1906 he was the author of six books – another 34 were to follow. Some of them, like *Great Contemporaries* (1937) were collections of articles for newspapers and magazines, to which Churchill was a frequent contributor between the wars: in 1934 alone he published 50 articles.

Churchill always lived by his pen. He needed to: a

English-speaking peoples".[84] He called for an alliance between the US and the British Empire in which weapons and strategy would be co-ordinated. The idea had a mixed reception. *The New York Times*, which paid tribute to Churchill as "the towering leader who guided the British Empire and indeed our whole civilization through their darkest hours", was broadly supportive. In *The Washington Post*, however, Walter Lippman argued that Churchill had failed to understand the enormous problems his proposal would cause for Americans. There could be no alliance between the States and a colonial empire: "That is not a workable argument to propose to a people as deeply imbued as the Americans with the tradition and the conviction that empires are at best a necessary evil, to be liquidated as soon as possible."[85]

minister's salary never covered more than a fraction of what it took to support his wife and children and staff of maidservants, secretaries, chauffeur and three gardeners, not to mention the magnums of champagne. The historian Peter Clarke has estimated that in the 1930s Churchill's literary earnings were the equivalent in today's terms of around £600,000 a year. It was never quite enough. "Churchill's system," writes Clarke, "depended on mortgaging the future to provide cash flow in the present."[86] He took huge advances from publishers and spent freely in the belief that he could always raise more if the money ran out, which it invariably did. In 1937 he was compelled to put his much loved home, Chartwell, on the market, only to be rescued at the last minute by a wealthy financier who took over his debts. ∎

Lippmann was right. No US government was prepared to extend a military guarantee to the entire British Empire. In the Suez crisis of 1956, when Britain invaded Egypt with the aim of overthrowing the dictatorship of Colonel Nasser, it was Churchill's old wartime ally, President Eisenhower, who forced the British into a humiliating withdrawal.

If the Iron Curtain speech was the first of Churchill's great contributions to the ordering of the post-war world, the other was the speech he delivered in Zurich in September 1946. He called for the reconciliation of France and Germany and the establishment of a united Europe, whilst stressing that the destinies of the British were separate from those of the Continental powers.

As he had written in 1930, when the idea of a united Europe was floated by the French politician Aristide Briand:

> We [Britain] are bound to further every honest and practical step which the nations of Europe may make to reduce the barriers which divide them and to nourish their common interests and their common welfare. We rejoice at every diminution of the internal tariffs and the martial armaments of Europe. We see nothing but good and hope in a richer, freer, more contented European commonalty. But we have our own

Opposite: The prime minister in 1940 during an attack on ramsgate

> dream and our own task. We are with Europe, but
> not of it. We are linked, but not comprised. We
> are interested and associated, but not absorbed.[87]

Churchill's Zurich speech gave a powerful impetus to the movement for a united Europe and he came to be regarded as one of its founding fathers. The main effects were felt outside rather than inside Britain, and most of all in assisting the reconciliation of France and Germany. But he also flirted with the idea of British participation in Europe. He accepted the leadership of the British European movement, an all-party pressure group organised by his son-in-law Duncan Sandys, and attacked the Labour government for failing to play a more constructive role in forging European unity.

The Attlee government took no part in the Hague Congress of 1948, called to discuss European political co-operation, but Churchill attended as honorary president. In 1950, at the opening session of the Council of Europe at Strasbourg, he successfully moved a resolution in favour of the creation of a European army and appeared to suggest that Britain would play a part in it. All this led has some observers to the mistaken conclusion that Churchill was a committed "European". In fact he never wavered from views he had expressed before the war. As he explained in a speech to the Conservative party conference in October 1948, Britain had a unique role to play as the link between "the three great circles among the free nations and democracies" – Britain and the Empire, the United States, and a united Europe.

Was Churchill a warmonger?

In the general election campaign of October 1951 the Labour party accused Churchill of being a "warmonger" and the pro-Labour Daily Mirror ran the headline "Whose Finger on the Trigger?"[88] His return to office, Labour claimed, would make a Third World War more likely. Churchill replied that the only reason he remained in public life was to try to prevent such a war and to bring nearer "that lasting peace settlement which the masses of the people of every race and in every land fervently desire".[89] On the Left, the issue was clouded by ideology. They remembered his attempts in 1919 to escalate the Allied war of intervention in Russia. They remembered, too, his use of troops in the national rail strike of 1911 and his allegedly hot-headed behaviour in the general strike of 1926.

Churchill himself worried that his love of war bordered on the pathological. A few days before the outbreak of war in 1914 he wrote to Clementine: 'Everything tends towards catastrophe and collapse. I am interested, geared-up & happy. Is it not horrible to be built like that? I pray to God to forgive me for such fearful moods of levity – Yet I wd do my best for peace, & nothing wd induce me wrongfully to strike the blow...'[90]

Apart from a small pacifist minority, the British generally accepted war as a normal means, if only in the last resort, of defending the national interest. In the circumstances of the Second World War Churchill's fighting spirit was generally regarded as providential. It was only after the war that the notion that he was too aggressive and brutal found expression. The great commanders of history had all been soldiers and sailors carrying out their professional duties; Churchill was a politician. The suspicion that he had promoted military operations for personal political gain could never be entirely dispelled. The memory of Churchill as a warlord was so pervasive that it blotted out the periods of his life in which he had been far from bellicose. Between 1900 and 1910 he was a frequent critic of greater expenditure on arms and warned against alarmism in international affairs. After World War One he again concentrated on cutting the defence budget. His peacetime government of 1951-5 was equally subject to Treasury constraints, cutting back on the rearmament programme authorised by the previous Labour government.

Writing in the 18th century the philosopher David Hume argued that human beings possessed in their make-up a "particle of the dove" along with the elements of the wolf and the serpent. In the late 1940s the wolf and the serpent all but overwhelmed the dove in Churchill. On a number of occasions he argued in private for a "showdown" with Russia while the United States still had a monopoly of nuclear weapons. In 1949, however, the Soviet Union exploded its own atom bomb, while the Americans, at the invitation of the Labour government, were establishing air bases in East Anglia that would place Britain in the front line of a nuclear exchange. Dismayed at the prospects for humanity as well as for his own country, Churchill resolved to take up the role of peacemaker. His last great mission, the dominant theme of his peacetime government of 1951-1955, was the prevention of nuclear war.

What did his final government achieve?

Churchill ought perhaps to have resigned the leadership of the Conservative Party, and with it the hope of a return to 10 Downing Street, in 1945. By 1951 he was 76 and no longer possessed the physical energy or the powers of mental concentration he had displayed during the war, "It is impossible", writes Roy Jenkins, "to re-read the story of Churchill's life as prime minister of that second government without feeling that he was gloriously unfit for office...The most important milestones of his political year were the occasions when he would endeavour to show the Cabinet or the Americans, the Conservative Conference or the House of Commons, that he was fit to carry on."[91]

As he was going deaf, Churchill had to be supplied with a hearing aid for Cabinet meetings. With the assistance of the Cabinet Secretary, Norman Brook, he chaired the Cabinet in his usual discursive style until June 1953, when he suffered a stroke which left him partially paralysed. He was out of action for two months but the nature of his

THE STATE FUNERAL

It was customary to honour a departed monarch with a state funeral but rare for a commoner. Since 1800 only four had been granted the privilege: Nelson, Wellington, Palmerston and Gladstone. Five years before his death Churchill was told that the Queen and the Prime Minister wished to accord him a state funeral. He consented and preparations began for "Operation Hope Not".

Churchill died at his home at Hyde Park Gate on the morning of Sunday 24 January 1965, 70 years to the day since the death of his father, Lord Randolph. His body lay in state in Westminster Hall for three days while more than 300,000 people filed past the coffin. On 30 January it was taken on a gun carriage to St Paul's Cathedral for a funeral service attended by 3,000 people including family, friends, wartime colleagues and commanders, four kings, one queen, 15 heads of state illness was concealed from the public by a secret circle of conspirators, led by R.A. Butler and Lord Salisbury, who doctored the medical bulletins and persuaded the press to collude in the fiction that Churchill was merely taking a rest. It had long been assumed that the Foreign Secretary, Anthony Eden, was his heir apparent, but Churchill was in luck. Eden was recuperating from a botched operation, and could not be sent for. Churchill, meanwhile, began to recover and by the autumn was well enough to return to work. On great occasions, like his speech to the Conservative

and representatives of 112 nations.

The coffin was then taken through the streets of the City to Tower Pier, where it was transferred to a Port of London launch. From Festival Pier the coffin was taken to Waterloo station and transferred to the locomotive "Winston Churchill" for the village of Bladon, Oxfordshire, where he was to be buried. The author, who was then a student at Oxford, was in the crowd that gathered to watch as the train passed slowly through Oxford station, the coffin draped in the Union Jack, a white-faced Randolph Churchill staring out from a carriage window. To me it felt as though we were back in a pre-Christian era, watching as some great tribal warrior was taken to his funeral pyre, with pagan magic in the air and the ground trembling beneath our feet. After a short private service in the parish church of the village of Bladon Churchill was buried in the churchyard next to his father, his mother, and his brother Jack.

The funeral ceremony was a brilliant pageant, watched around the world on television, and understood almost everywhere to symbolise the end of the British Empire and, perhaps, the end of a ruling class. ∎

Party conference at Blackpool in October, he could still rise to the occasion, but his political life hung by a thread.

In domestic affairs he sought a quiet life. There was no counter-revolution against the collectivist reforms of the Labour government, though some changes were made. Steel was denationalised, the BBC deprived of its monopoly of television. As international trade recovered and the supply of scarce commodities increased, a multitude of economic controls was scrapped, and food rationing ended in 1954. Churchill, however. had no wish to pull down the pillars of the new welfare state – the National Health Service, the social security system, and public sector housing. He gave strong support to his Minister of Housing, Harold Macmillan, in fulfilling the Conservative promise to build 300,000 houses a year. With the aim of appeasing the trade unions and avoiding strikes, he instructed his Minister of Labour, Walter Monckton, to accept inflationary wage settlements if necessary.

In foreign affairs Churchill's first priority was the re-establishment of the Anglo-American "special relationship". In January 1952 he crossed the Atlantic for discussions with President Truman. Outwardly relations were full of bonhomie, but the President and his advisers did not share Churchill's conception of a global alliance and rejected his pleas for American military support in the Suez Canal zone. When Eisenhower was elected in November 1952, Churchill hastened to the US again, for consultations with his former comrade-in-arms. But greatly though Eisenhower admired Churchill, he thought his view of Anglo-American relations sentimental and privately concluded that he was living in the past. Churchill's pleas for diplomatic support over Egypt were rejected. Nor did "Ike" warm to Churchill's idea of a summit conference with the Russians.

Although Churchill pressed repeatedly for discussions with the Kremlin, he never defined the terms of the settlement he was seeking. There is no doubt that his last great ambition was to play the role of peacemaker, and with the death of Stalin on 5 March 1953 his hopes of *détente* rose. In December 1953 Eisenhower attended a conference in Bermuda at Churchill's invitation, but again rejected his proposals for a common approach to Russia. When Churchill flew to Washington in June 1954, however, Eisenhower was more amenable, even agreeing that Churchill should go alone to Moscow. But Churchill overplayed his hand, dispatching, a telegram to Molotov, the Russian Minister of Foreign Affairs, on his return voyage without consulting the Cabinet. The consequence, when he got home, was a Cabinet crisis in which he was strongly opposed by Eden and other senior ministers.

Churchill, of course, was no unilateral disarmer. It was under his chairmanship that the Defence Committee of the Cabinet decided in June 1954 to recommend that Britain build its hydrogen bomb as a deterrent against Soviet attack. Churchill also grasped the fact that with both the United States and the Soviet Union in possession of nuclear weapons, the world now stood on the brink of self-destruction. His last major speech in the Commons (1 March 1955) was devoted to the dangers of a nuclear holocaust but ended on a note of hope: "It may well be that we shall, by a process of sublime irony, have reached a stage where safety will be the sturdy shield of terror, and survival the twin brother of annihilation."[92]

Conclusion: the Churchill Myth

Like all the most interesting myths in history the "Churchill Myth" was true in part, which is one reason why so many historians and biographers still pay tribute to him. The Myth, however, was at its weakest in the insistence of his greatest admirers that he was always, or nearly always, right. In the six volumes of The Second World War Churchill was determined to vindicate his own judgment and as long as he possessed a near monopoly of the historical sources his claims were hard to dispute. With the passage of time the monopoly broke down, exposing weaknesses and mistakes – along with other revelations that were greatly to his credit.

The psychiatrist Anthony Storr put forward the hypothesis that Churchill matched one of the personality types defined by Jung, the "extroverted intuitive". According to Jung:

> The intuitive is never to be found among the generally recognized reality values, but is always present where possibilities exist. He has a keen nose for things in the bud pregnant with future promise... thinking and feeling, the indispensable components of conviction, are, with him, inferior functions, possessing no decisive weight: hence

they lack the power to offer any lasting resistance to the force of intuition.

Though frequently regarded as ruthless and immoral, Jung continued, "his capacity to inspire his fellow-men with courage, or to kindle enthusiasm for something new, is unrivalled".[93]

Testimony from people who worked with Churchill lends strong support to Storr's hypothesis. As Roosevelt put it, he had a hundred ideas every day, four of which were good. To put such a man in a position where he could intervene at will in military operations and grand strategy was a hazardous experiment. Readers should ask themselves: would I have been happy to take part in an amphibious operation masterminded by Churchill? In a sense there was logic behind the whispering campaign, early in 1942, to deprive him of the role of Minister of Defence, and he should not be let off the hook because he made fine speeches defending his actions.

The attempt to show that Churchill was almost always a fount of wisdom – or that someone else was to blame if things went wrong – has been steadily undermined by historians. The truth is that his judgment was highly variable, but it was leadership rather than judgment that marked him out as head and shoulders above his contemporaries. Courage, energy, determination, eloquence and pugnacity were his greatest qualities, and he deployed them in the setting of goals, the raising of morale, the infusion of drive into the government machine, the establishment of personal relations with Roosevelt and Stalin, the half-conscious creation of the dramatic illusions necessary to get him and the British through the war. To have provided such leadership in three different spheres, as the leader of a democracy, as a military leader, and as the lynchpin of the Anglo-American and Anglo-Soviet alliances, was a phenomenal achievement. All three roles were harmonised by the absolute clarity of his objective: military victory over Nazi Germany.

Some historians believe that the cost was too high, but it would have been much higher if Britain had been defeated and Hitler left in uncontested control of Western Europe, followed perhaps by a victorious campaign in Russia. By some extraordinary conjunction of circumstances, a Churchill was needed and a Churchill was found. He was not only a great man, but one of the most astonishing and fortunate accidents in British and world history.

A SHORT CHRONOLOGY

1874 30 November Churchill born at Blenheim Palace.

1888-94 Harrow and then Sandhurst, from which he passes out 20th in a class of 120.

1895 Commissioned in the 4th Queen's own Hussars. Serves in Bangalore, on the North West Frontier (now part of Pakistan), and with Kitchener's expedition to the Sudan. Works simultaneously as a newspaper reporter.

1899 Resigns from the army and sails for the Cape to report on the war in South Africa. On 15 November he is captured and imprisoned by the Boers. A month later he escapes.

1900 After a brief spell back in the army, combining his duties again with those of a war correspondent, he is elected Tory MP for Oldham.

1904-05 Churchill "crosses the floor" to join the Liberals, becoming Parliamentary Under-Secretary at the Colonial Office.

1906-10 President of the Board of Trade and then, in 1910, Home Secretary. In November 1910 he sends forces to prevent rioting in Tonypandy in Wales.

1911 First Lord of the Admiralty.

1914 4 August Britain declares war on Germany.

1915 The navy attacks the Dardanelles, followed by Allied landings on the Gallipoli peninsular. Churchill is blamed for a disastrous campaign and in May is demoted to Chancellor of the Duchy of Lancaster. In July he takes up what becomes a long-term hobby: oil painting. In November he resigns from the